FLEETBOOK

Buses of OUTER LONDON
3rd edition 1986

Edited and published by
A M WITTON
Room 20 City Buildings
69 Corporation Street
Manchester M4 2DE

Copyright 1986 by A M Witton
ISBN 0 86047 163 2 - 3rd edition revised and enlarged 1986
(ISBN 0 86047 161 6 - 1st edition 1979)
(ISBN 0 86047 162 4 - 2nd edition revised 1981)

ABC Taxis
(J Lambley) Ltd

Blue Saloon Coaches was started in 1924 by A T Locke & Son from Stoke Road, Guildford - near the present ABC Taxis office. Blue Saloon ran from Guildford to Ripley, Send and Woking, with Ford, Dodge and Guy vehicles. The operating area was partly within the LPTB's area from 1933, but Aldershot & District made a takeover bid in 1937, representing LPTB as well as itself. The two big firms took over on 12th January 1938, sharing the buses and services between themselves.

Mr J Lambley was one of Mr Locke's drivers, but left to work for another firm which pioneered the forerunner of the present 715 Green Line service. After a spell with LPTB, Mr Lambley founded ABC Taxis in 1945. In May 1961 the first full-sized PSVs were bought, and they soon became the main activity. Mr Lambley acquired the right to use the Blue Saloon name, and this became the fleetname of ABC Taxis' coaching fleet, although the two companies were not connected otherwise.

On 1st March 1973 Blue Saloon started a bus service between Guildford and Merrow (Boxgrove Park), after Blue Saloon, Tillingbourne and London Country had each argued for the right to run the service. It was later extended to Woodbridge Meadows west of Guildford, serving a small area remote from any main road. Later a new service from Charlotteville to Woodbridge Meadows was added. Three London RF-type buses were bought for the stage services, but the Company parted with the last of these in October 1985; Bristol LH buses are nowadays normally used on the stage services. Blue and white livery is used.

On 14th April 1985 Blue Saloon increased its stage network after tendering, with Safeguard and Tillingbourne, to work former NBC routes. The old service 1 (Guildford and Boxgrove Park) has become G1, with an extension to Onslow Village on the other side of Guildford, formerly served by Alder Valley. The Charlotteville and Woodbridge Meadows route is extended to Grange Park Estate as service G2; the Grange Park section, formerly served by Alder Valley only, is shared by Blue Saloon and Alder Valley, but the latter does not work on the Charlotteville side. Blue Saloon also runs service 3, an occasional Fridays-only service from Guildford to Woking, with extensions to Slyfield Market.

Regn. Number	Chassis Make and Type	Body Make and Seats	Date New	Notes
1131 VY	Leyland 'Royal Tiger'	Van Hool C53F	1985	
776 WME	Leyland 'Royal Tiger' B54	Roe C46FT	1984	
OJH 301D	Bedford VAM14	Plaxton C37F	1966	(a)
DHW 291K	Bristol LH6L	ECW B42F	1972	(b)
DHW 292K	"	"	"	(c)
ORO 311L	Seddon 'Pennine' Mk VI	Plaxton C49F	1973	(d)
UCO 43L	Leyland National 1151/2R	B46D	"	(e)
KJD 427P	Bristol LH6L	ECW B39F	1976	(f)
KPB 881P	"	ECW B43F	1975	
KPM 429P	"	Plaxton C45F	"	
OPC 24R	Bedford YMT	Plaxton C53F	1976	(g)
VRY 724S	"	"	1978	(g)
VDV 107S	Bristol LH6L	ECW B43F	"	(h)
YPB 820T	Bedford YMT	Plaxton C53F	"	
YPH 406T	"	"	"	
YPH 407T	"	"	"	

Regn. Number	Chassis Make and Type	Body Make and Seats	Date New	Notes
CPD 131T	Bristol LH6L	ECW B43F	1979	
HPB 814V	Bedford YMT	Plaxton C53F	1980	
KPC 405W	"	Duple C53F	"	(g)
RPE 556X	Leyland 'Tiger' TRCTL11/3R	Plaxton C53F	1981	
WLP 958X	Bedford CFS	Dormobile 12-seat	1982	
HBH 426Y	Leyland 'Tiger' TRCTL11/3R	Plaxton C53F	1983	
XPG 295Y	DAF MB200DKTL600	Plaxton C57F	1982	(g)

NOTES:-
(a) OJH 301D was ex Capital, London W1, in 1972
(b) DHW 291K was ex Gable Hall School, Corringham (non-PSV) in 1985
(c) DHW 292K was ex Bristol Omnibus Co No. 352 in 1981
(d) ORO 311L was ex Cavalier, London SW17, in 1977
(e) UCO 43L was ex Plymouth City Transport No. 43 in 1980
(f) KJD 427P was ex London Buses Ltd No. BL27 in 1985; as we went to press in October 1985 it had not yet been repainted in Blue Saloon service
(g) OPC 24R, VRY 724S, KPC 405W and XPG 295Y were ex Warner, Milford, in 1983
(h) VDV 107S was ex Devon General No. 127 in 1985

Banstead Coaches Ltd

The late Mr A E Pullen founded a haulage business in 1946, and one year later he went into partnership with Mr C F Haynes. They bought a secondhand Bedford OB coach in 1950, and soon began to trade as 'Banstead Coaches'. By 1954 the fleet had grown to four vehicles, and in 1958 a Limited Company was incorporated.

At the end of 1958 another secondhand Bedford OB was bought, with a Mulliner bus body, to start a bus service between Banstead and Chipstead Valley via the previously busless village of Woodmansterne. The bus entered service in pink and ivory livery - most previous vehicles had worn a blue livery - and the locals nicknamed it 'Candy Floss'. The service started in 1959 and was one of the first postwar independent stage services in the London area. It prospered and eventually bigger buses, Bedford SBs and later YRQs, were bought for it.

In 1964 Banstead Coaches took over London Transport service 263 between Coulsdon and Clock House Estate (The Mount). LT had worked this on Saturdays only, with a 2-hour break for the bus and its two-man crew to travel five miles to Croydon garage for a relief. Banstead Coaches worked the service with one-man Bedfords on a one-way loop route, serving a wider area than LT had done. It ran on Mondays to Saturdays from early morning to mid-evening. At first journeys from Coulsdon to the Foxley Lane area were interworked, but these were soon withdrawn. In June 1980, the Clock House route itself was abandoned by Banstead Coaches; since then it has been worked in turn by Tandridge Taxis Ltd of Coulsdon and by Guards Coaches of Caterham, both of whom have used smaller-type vehicles for it.

Banstead Coaches' vehicles have mainly been Bedfords, although there have been oddities such as a Commer 'Avenger', a Crossley SD42/7, a Leyland 'Tiger' TS4 which lasted only three months in the fleet, and a Trojan minibus which later went to Wallasey Corporation. Three Fords were bought new in 1960/1961, but all had been withdrawn by 1962. A couple of DAF coaches have been bought in the last few years. It is pleasing to note that the Company's workshops are busy restoring a Bedford OB coach, like the ones on which Banstead Coaches relied in the early days, to running order and hopefully PSV status; it is MYA 525, which spent most of its life with Wake's Coaches of Sparkford, Somerset.

Coaching work is by far the Company's main activity, and the awards from many British coach rallies bear testimony to this. However, the Company has earned much local goodwill with its stage bus services. The head office and garage is at Shrublands Road, Banstead, and the livery is pink and ivory.

Regn. Number	Chassis Make and Type	Body Make and Seats	Date New	Notes
GPA 846N	Bedford YRQ	Plaxton B45F	1974	(a)
VOR 813N	"	Plaxton C45F	"	
BYA 863S	Bedford CFS	Dormobile 12-seat	1978	
TPJ 272S	Bedford YMT	Van Hool McArdle C53F	1977	
APH 520T	"	Plaxton C53F	1979	
XDY 942T	"	Plaxton C49F	"	(b)
GPA 605V	"	Plaxton C53F	1980	
OLJ 192W	Bedford YNT	"	1981	
UJT 989X	"	"	1982	
BPA 370Y	DAF MB200DKTL600	"	1983	
YFX 181Y	"	"	1982	
A730 JAY	Bedford YMT	Plaxton C46F	1984	(c)
A212 PKK	Talbot	Rootes 12-seat	"	

NOTES:-
(a) GPA 846N was ex Tillingbourne, Gomshall, in 1982
(b) XDY 942T was ex Waterhouse, Polegate, No. 42 in 1984
(c) YFX 181Y was ex Tedd, Thruxton, in 1985

S G and R D Biss

The 'Biss Brothers' name has been used for two separate periods of bus operation, by two generations of the same family, completely separated both in space and time! The first began on November 30th 1923, when Messrs J S, R W and P R Biss began to run two Straker-Squire buses from their Waltham Cross base under the 'BB' fleetname. The fleet grew to 13 buses, both single and double-deck, but the first Straker-Squires later buses were Dennises. The routes included a marathon Sundays-only service from the Elephant & Castle to Hertford. This caused the firm trouble with the National company – the major operators in Hertford – and with several local councils at the rural end of the route.

The firm was sold to the London Public Omnibus Co on May 31st 1927, after becoming a limited company in 1924 – the only time that the Biss family's bus operations have ever had company status. The family left the bus industry altogether, and 'Public' passed their routes and vehicles over, to the LGOC in March 1928. The Biss name did not re-appear on buses until 1950, when S G and R D Biss, the next generation of the family, took over the business of H Monk of Bishop's Stortford, with nine vehicles and several stage licences. They tried to re-establish themselves at Waltham Cross, by introducing a service from Waltham Abbey to Roydon using a Bedford OB in 1952. However, this was not a success and was withdrawn.

Several double-deckers have been owned during the Bishop's Stortford era, but nowadays the fleet is all single-deck, of a variety of makes. The stage services run from Bishop's Stortford to Furneaux Pelham (daily except Sundays), Farnham

Green (Tuesdays and Thursdays) and Birchanger (Thursdays); they require only one vehicle, normally nowadays a Bedford YRQ coach. A major activity is the operation of foreign tours for schools, and conventional touring is also operated. The fleet is liveried in blue and white. The head office was at Sun Garage, Rye Street, Bishop's Stortford, from 1950 until October 1984, when Biss Brothers moved to London Road, Spellbrook, near Bishops Stortford.

Regn. Number	Chassis Make and Type	Body Make and Seats	Date New	Notes
PJH 457H	AEC 'Reliance' 6U3ZR	Plaxton C51F	1970	
PJH 458H	"	"	"	
CRO 686K	Bedford YRQ	Plaxton C45F	1972	
CRO 687K	"	Plaxton C41F	"	
CRO 688K	AEC 'Reliance' 6U3ZR	Plaxton C51F	"	
HVD 735N	Volvo B58-61	"	1975	
JVS 935N	Bedford YRQ	Plaxton C45F	"	
PNK 160R	Leyland 'Leopard' PSU5A/4R	Van Hool C50F	1976	
KBH 860V	Leyland 'Leopard' PSU5C/4R	Plaxton C57F	1980	
KBH 861V	"	Plaxton C51F	"	
UEV 249M	Mercedes-Benz 508D	Whittaker C19F	1981	
FOO 650Y	Mercedes-Benz O303/15R	Jonckheere C52FT	1982	
GHJ 568Y	"	Jonckheere C51FT	1983	
GHJ 569Y	"	"	"	
A113 SNH	"	"	1984	
B423 CMC	Mercedes-Benz L608D	Reeves Burgess C19F	1985	(a)
B265 CVW	"	"	"	
B858 KRY	Bova 'Futura' FHM12-280	Bova C49FT	"	

NOTES:-
(a) B423 CMC was ex Pilcher, Bishops Stortford, in 1985, but may not have operated for Pilcher

Bordabus/ Bordacoach

In August 1958 LT route 238, from Noak Hill to Upminster (Woodhall Crescent), was withdrawn, to be replaced by Sterling Bus Service of Romford. After a few months operation was transferred to Super Coaches of Upminster. Soon the original route became four, linking Upminster, Hornchurch, County Park Estate and Gidea Park Station. Super Coaches acquired a substantial fleet; their fleet-numbering system suggested a bigger fleet still! The ex-Sterling services were operated under the 'Upminster and District' and 'Redbridge and District' fleetnames. The first double-deckers came in 1962; Super thereafter bought a wide variety of double-deckers, including many of ex-London Transport RT and RTL types. There was a close link with Passenger Vehicle Sales Ltd, the Upminster dealers, and buses in PVS stock often appeared on short-term loan to Super Coaches.

In February 1969 Super Coaches (Upminster) Ltd was acquired by PVS (Holdings) Ltd, along with "Upminster & District" which had latterly been owned personally by Mr R W Wordsworth, a director of Super Coaches. The 40 vehicles and the services were passed to City Coach Lines (Upminster) Ltd. In June 1971 most of the City Coach Lines business, including 26 vehicles, was transferred to Blue Line Coaches Ltd. All of these firms used a garage near Upminster Bridge LT station. Late in 1973 Coppin's Coaches (proprietor, Mr W R Thompson) set up in business at Havering-atte-Bower, north of Romford, and became the fifth operator of the

Upminster/County Park/Gidea Park local network.

Mr G F Stubbington started trading as 'Dorayme Travel' in May 1975, and took Mr M J Williams into partnership in June 1976; at about the same time the Romford/Upminster area services were transferred to them. By now the services were numbered 1-4, all radiating from County Park Estate and going to Gidea Park Station (1, Mon-Fri), Hornchurch (White Hart) (2, Mon-Sat), Upminster Bridge Station (3, two journeys Mon-Fri) and Langton School (4, school journeys only on Mon-Fri). In May 1977 Mr Williams left the partnership, and Mr Stubbington arranged with Lewington's Coach Hire to garage vehicles in their Abridge yard. From 1981 Lewington's and Mr Stubbington adopted the name 'Bordabus' for both firms' services in the Essex/Greater London border area; in December 1981 Bordabus Ltd was set up to work the bus services, with Lewington's and Mr Stubbington's 'Dorayme Travel' doing their own contract and private hire work.

In March 1982 Lewington's Coach Hire Services Ltd went into liquidation, and Bordabus Ltd took over further vehicles from the Lewington's fleet. One of these was PPF 779E, a Bedford VAS with one of the last Thurgood bodies to be built, but this was withdrawn after a few months with the new firm. Bordabus also took over the Dorayme services and the newer routes built up over the previous few years.

In March 1984 these services and vehicles passed back to the personal control of Mr Stubbington, who still trades as 'Dorayme', 'Bordabus' and 'Bordacoach' although 'Boardacoach' is the fleetname on most vehicles. By early 1985 the original County Park routes had been reduced to service 1 (County Park to Gidea Park Station) (Mondays to Fridays, peak periods only), and service 4 (school journeys for Langton's School and Campion School). Other routes include 6 (Abridge to Brentwood) with six round trips on Mondays to Fridays only; 8 (Cheshunt and Romford) with three round trips on Wednesdays and Saturdays, and one on Fridays; and several coastal and shopping journeys, numbered 9 (Cheshunt and Southend-on-Sea), 16 (Cheshunt and Maidstone) and 17 (Brentwood and Milton Keynes). These run weekly (9) or alternate weeks (16 and 17) during the summer season only.

The head office is at Mr Stubbington's home at Highview Road, Thundersley Common, Benfleet; the garage and traffic office are at Patch Park, Abridge. Red and white livery is used; some vehicles are operated in 'as acquired' liveries at times. Mr Stubbington also owns a 1956 vintage AEC 'Reliance' with Burlingham Seagull bodywork, which it is intended to restore to original condition.

Fleet No.	Regn. Number	Chassis Make and Type	Body Make and Seats	Date New	Notes
62	GMF 709J	Leyland 'Leopard' PSU3B/4R	Plaxton C51F	1971	(a)
63	GMF 703J	Leyland 'Leopard' PSU5/4R	Plaxton C55F	"	(a)
69	UFN 482H	AEC 'Reliance' 6U3ZR	Duple Northern C40F	1970	(b)
70	524 FN	AEC 'Reliance' 2U3RA	Plaxton C49F	1962	(c)
77	XVY 692J	Daimler 'Fleetline' CRC6LX	Roe H44/34F	1971	(d)
80	RCU 280S	Bedford VAS5	Plaxton C29F	1977	(e)

NOTES:-
(a) 62/63 (GMF 709/703J) were ex British Airways Nos. CC82/C076 in 1982
(b) 69 (UFN 482H) was ex East Kent Road Car Co No. 8482 in 1982
(c) 70 (524 FN) was ex East Kent Road Car Co No. 8524 in 1982; the body was new in 1972, and the vehicle originally carried Park Royal bodywork
(d) 77 (XVY 692J) was ex York Pullman Bus Co., York, No. 92, in 1985
(e) 80 (RCU 280S) was ex Priory, North Shields, in 1985

British Airways Board

In 1946 two State-owned airlines, BEA and BOAC, were formed out of the pre-war Imperial Airways. Their main base was moved to the ex-RAF base at Heathrow on the Great West Road, although several other airports (e.g. Croydon, Stansted and Blackbushe) were used for a while. BEA had a Northolt base until the early 1950s.

The airlines had to organise road transport for passengers from Heathrow and the other airports to various points in central London. They operated frequent coach services for air passengers between Heathrow and the London terminals. BEA used a terminal on the South Bank near Waterloo Station until 1957, when they moved to the West London Air Terminal at Cromwell Road, Kensington. BOAC built a terminal at Buckingham Palace Road, Victoria, opposite Victoria Coach Station. Both airlines ran regular services at busy times, and met specified flights at other times. Passengers either paid on the coach or bought tickets at the terminal.

A variety of vehicles was used on these services. Both airlines started with small vehicles, Bedford OBs and Commer 'Commandos', the latter fitted with Park Royal 23-seat 'observation deck' bodies. Larger coaches were soon required for the increasing numbers of air passengers. BEA agreed with London Transport for LT to operate 65 coaches on AEC 'Regal' Mk IV chassis for BEA; these were mechanically similar to LT's 'RF' class although 8 ft wide, but the bodywork was of 'observation deck' layout by Park Royal. There was a large luggage boot beneath the raised rear seats, and a total seating capacity of 37. An experimental double-deck AEC 'Regent' Mk V coach came in 1961, and after experience with this vehicle a fleet of AEC 'Routemasters' arrived in 1966/1967 to replace the 'Regals'. They were specially built to BEA design, and hauled two-wheeled luggage trailers. The last 'Routemasters' were withdrawn following cessation of British Airways' Heathrow - London service; many were sold to London Transport, mostly for use as staff buses and for driver training. All the 'BEA' fleet from the Regals onwards were operated for BEA, and later for British Airways, by London Transport under contract; LT provided staff, garages and maintenance facilities. The vehicles were however owned by the airline, and were not strictly part of the LT fleet.

BOAC used Commer-Harringtons, Bedford SBs and finally Leyland 'Atlanteans' (with large luggage compartments) for the busier workings. The 'Atlanteans' were withdrawn like BEA's 'Routemasters', and the British Airways fleet has been wholly single-deck since then. BOAC also bought some Karrier 'Bantams' about 1960, mainly for transfer of airline staff within the Heathrow area; these have been replaced by Leyland 'Redlines', Bedford VAS and most recently Bristol LHS coaches.

In 1962, both airlines acquired the duty to provide 'airside' transport for passengers changing between flights. The 'airside' buses run from one loading area to another within the Customs-controlled area, and they are therefore rarely on view to the public unless when parked. As they do not use public roads, they are not subject to PSV design rules, and a wide variety of types has been tried. These included the articulated unit, with a tractor pulling a semi-trailer with seats for 50 and standing room for many more. One-piece 'airside' buses have been built on Bedford VAL and more recently Leyland National chassis. The articulated concept has lately been re-introduced, in the form of DAB/Leyland National 'bendibuses', of which seven are now in stock. All 'airside' buses have centre doors on both sides, and many also have a forward nearside entrance opposite the driver.

In September 1973, BEA and BOAC were merged into the British Airways Board, the two airlines becoming the European and Overseas Divisions respectively. At first, little change took place in coach operation; the Divisions continued to run from their own London terminals, with their different vehicle types. The main change was the replacement of BEA's grey/off-white and BOAC's blue/grey liveries with a handsome new navy blue and white scheme, with the 'British Airways' emblem and fleetname. Later, the two Divisions were merged operationally, and all motor vehicles owned by the airline carry fleet numbers based on the old BEA system; buses carry numbers prefixed by 'BU', whilst coaches carry a 'CC' prefix.

After the Piccadilly Line tube was extended to Heathrow Central, the airline coach fleets lost much of their traffic between the airport and central London. From April 1st 1979 the West London Air Terminal was closed, and services ran from the former BOAC terminal at Victoria. There was a brief increase in traffic at Victoria after this move, but the traffic decline continued, and in 1980 British Airways decided that the London coach service was uneconomic and would have to go; the ageing double-deck coaches could not be economically replaced for a shrinking operation. From 15th November 1980 London Transport started two new 'Airbus' services linking Heathrow to Victoria (service A1) and Paddington/West London (service A2); they have since been joined by a third, from Heathrow to Euston (service A3). The 'Airbuses' are purpose-built 'Metrobuses' with built-in luggage bins on the lower deck, one for each of the three Heathrow terminals. Unlike the LT/BEA agreement, these Metrobuses are owned and operated directly by LT, and thus British Airways no longer runs public coach services into central London.

British Airways also owns a large and assorted fleet of vehicles at its many bases in the UK and abroad. The following list should include all vehicles of PSV type (although the 'airside' fleet is not PSV licensed) based at Heathrow. There are also, of course, many cars, vans, lorries and other specialised non-passenger carrying vehicles used at Heathrow and elsewhere.

Finally, a warning. This description of the British Airways bus and coach fleet is mainly for interest's sake, as many of the vehicles are not normally on public view. At Heathrow Airport, for many reasons, security needs to be tightly enforced. Readers must therefore keep within those areas of the Airport open to the public. There is no public access to areas where British Airways garages or maintains its vehicles, or to the 'airside' except for passengers transferring between flights.

BU040-048
CC049-053

Chassis and Body: Leyland National 11351A/1R integral construction vehicles with B33 triple-door (nearside front and centre, offside centre) bodies (C049/C051 are B29 triple-door), built 1978
CC049-053 are used as courtesy buses for the Heathrow - Gatwick Helicopter Link service; the others are 'airside' buses not licensed as PSVs
CC051/053 were originally registered WGY 598/596S and were re-registered in 1980

BU040	WGY 583S	BU043	WGY 586S	BU046	WGY 589S	CC050	WGY 595S
BU041	WGY 584S	BU044	WGY 587S	BU048	WGY 593S	CC051	EGT 458T
BU042	WGY 585S	BU045	WGY 588S	CC049	WGY 594S	CC053	EGT 460T

BU120-123

Chassis and Body: Leyland National 11351A/3R integral-construction vehicles with B33 triple-door (nearside front and centre, offside centre) bodies, built 1977
These 'airside' buses are not licensed as PSVs

| BU120 | TBY 114R | BU123 | TBY 126R |

CC141-156

Chassis: Bedford VAS5 built 1978
Body: Duple C24F

| CC141 | DLA 923T | CC143 | DLA 918T | CC146 | DLA 918T | CC148 | CMJ 459T |
| CC142 | DLA 922T | CC144 | DLA 920T | CC147 | DLA 917T | CC149 | CMJ 458T |

CC150	CMJ 457T	CC153	CMJ 454T	CC155	CMJ 452T	CC156	CMJ 451T
CC151	CMJ 456T	CC154	CMJ 453T				

BU168-175

Chassis and Body: Leyland National 11351A/3R integral-construction vehicles with B33 triple-door (nearside front and centre, offside centre) bodies, built 1979
These 'airside' buses are not licensed as PSVs

BU168	GLP 422T	BU170	GLP 428T	BU172	GLP 433T	BU174	HLY 523V
BU169	GLP 427T	BU171	GLP 431T	BU173	HLD 30T	BU175	HLY 524V

BU278-280

Chassis and Body: Leyland National 2 115L11/3R. integral-construction vehicles with B33 triple-door (nearside front and centre, offside centre) bodies, built 1980
These 'airside' buses are not licensed as PSVs

BU278 NLP 388V   BU279 NLP 391V   BU280 NLP 389V

CC300-304

Chassis: Bristol LHS6L built 1980
Body: Plaxton C26F

CC300	RLN 227W	CC302	RLN 229W	CC303	RLN 230W	CC304	RLN 231W
CC301	RLN 228W						

BU305-311

Chassis and Body: DAB articulated running units with Roe/Leyland National AB45 triple-door (nearside front and centre, offside centre) bodies, built 1981
These 'airside' buses are not licensed as PSVs

BU305	RLN 232W	BU307	RLN 234W	BU309	RLN 236W	EU311	RLN 238W
BU306	RLN 233W	BU308	RLN 235W	BU310	RLN 237W		

CC312-317

Chassis: Leyland 'Tiger' TRCTL11/2R built 1981/1982
Body: Plaxton C53F

CC312	VOY 179X	CC314	VOY 181X	CC316	VOY 183X	CC317	VOY 184X
CC313	VOY 180X	CC315	VOY 182X				

BU390-393

Chassis: Ford/Tricentrol R1014 built 1982
Body: Lex B20 triple-door (nearside front and centre, offside centre) with perimeter seating
These 'airside' buses are not licensed as PSVs

BU390 WLF 59X   BU391 WLF 60X   BU392 WLF 61X   BU393 WLF 62X

A963 CUX

Chassis: Quest 80B built 1984
Body: Locomotors B32F
Received on long-term loan from the manufacturers in 1984 - no fleet number is carried

A963 CUX

BU394-399

Chassis and Body: Leyland National 2 NL116TL11/1R integral-construction vehicles with B33 triple-door (nearside front and centre, offside centre) bodies, built 1984
These 'airside' buses are not licensed as PSVs

BU394	B358 LOY	BU396	B360 LOY	BU398	B362 LOY	BU399	B363 LOY
BU395	B359 LOY	BU397	B361 LOY				

BU8001-8002   Chassis: Ford R1014 built 1981
Body: Duple B29D
Ex National Car Parks, London W1, in 1984

BU8001   PNM 697W   BU8002   PNM 698W

CC8003-8008   Chassis: Leyland 'Tiger' TRCTL11/3R built 1985
Body: Plaxton C57F

CC8003	B413 CMC	CC8005	B415 CMC	CC8007	B417 CMC	CC8008	B412 CMC
CC8004	B414 CMC	CC8006	B416 CMC				

Camden Coaches Ltd

Camden Coaches is one of many firms which have taken over withdrawn NBC services on the fringe of the London Country area. Camden's home town, Sevenoaks (where the garage is an arch underneath the main Sevenoaks - London railway line) has long been a boundary point between London Country and Maidstone & District.

Camden Coaches was founded before the Second World War by the licensee of the "Camden Arms" public house. Shortly after the war it was taken over by Mr A J Boakes of Bosville Road, Sevenoaks, who ran a small fleet including some double-deckers. Two of the latter and a Commer "Avenger" coach were passed to the present business owned by Mr C Gillett, still trading as "Camden Coaches". He traded as sole proprietor from September 1974 until January 1978, when the firm was incorporated as Camden Coaches Ltd; at this stage the fleet consisted of four vehicles including an ex-Nottingham Daimler 'Fleetline' double-decker. In 1979 the business of Goddard of Ightham was acquired, with three vehicles.

Camden Coaches runs ex-Maidstone & District service 68, between Sevenoaks and Plaxtol via Godden Green. Three journeys are operated daily from Monday to Friday, and on Wednesdays and Fridays two trips extend to Dunks Green and Shipbourne. Several school journeys are also operated, bringing the total service to five or six round trips daily. There are no buses on weekends or Bank Holidays.

The headquarters address is The Arch, Morewood Close, Sevenoaks.

Regn. Number	Chassis Make and Type	Body Make and Seats	Date New	Notes
900 SAF	AEC 'Reliance' 2U3RA	Harrington C47F	1963	(a)
GUR 484L	Leyland 'Leopard' PSU3B/4R	Plaxton C51F	1972	(b)
GLJ 492N	Bristol LH6L	ECW B43F	1975	(c)
JAP 441N	Bedford YRQ	Duple C45F	"	(d)
JVS 930N	Bedford YRT	Plaxton C53F	"	(e)
KGT 895N	Bristol LHS6L	Plaxton C33F	"	(f)
XPE 125N	Ford 'Transit'	Dormobile B16F	1974	(g)
UGK 228R	Bristol LHS6L	Plaxton C33F	1977	
HNJ 973V	Bedford YMT	Plaxton C53F	1979	(h)
SLH 3W	Volvo B58-61	"	1981	(i)
B552 AKE	Mercedes-Benz L608D	Reeves Burgess C21F	1985	

NOTES:-
(a) 900 SAF was ex Killick & Vincent, Dallington, in 1974
(b) GUR 484L was ex Killick & Vincent, Dallington, in 1978
(c) GLJ 492N was ex Hants & Dorset Motor Services No. 3560 in 1982

(d) JAP 441N was ex Warren (Kent & Sussex), Ticehurst, in 1980
(e) JVS 930N was ex Sonner, Gillingham, in 1979
(f) KGT 895N and UCK 228R were ex Richmond, Epsom, in 1981/1982 respectively
(g) XPE 125N was ex Midland Red Omnibus Co No. 2125 in 1980
(h) HNJ 973V was ex Killick & Vincent, Dallington, in 1982
(i) SLH 3W was ex Albatross, Isleworth, in 1984

Charles Cook Coaches

Charles Cook founded this enterprise in June 1947 with a secondhand Dennis 'Ace', with a 20-seat bus body, from the Northern Ireland Road Transport Board. This was soon joined by a Dodge, also built pre-war but with coach bodywork. From them on Cook's concentrated on coaching; in July 1951 a Bedford OB left for a seven-day tour to Paris, and since then the excursions and tours business has steadily expanded. Cook's now offers extended tours ranging from the British Isles to Eastern Europe. Also operated is an express service from the Biggleswade area to the Thanet Coast resorts in Kent.

From 1972, Cook's bought several secondhand double-deckers; the present ones are four ex-London Transport buses, one DMS-type 'Fleetline' and three Scania 'Metropolitans' of the MD class. They run a Biggleswade - Stevenage bus route along the Great North Road, with a deviation through Stotfold. Although the two towns are linked by rail, the bus service is useful to the many villages which lie away from the railway line. Buses run once daily on Mondays to Fridays, with two through journeys and three 'shorts' each way on Saturdays.

The firm was formerly based at Mr Cook's house in Potton Road, Biggleswade. However, these premises have been vacated and a spacious new garage has been built at Langford Road, Biggleswade; the head office is at 59 High Street, Biggleswade. The livery is brown, beige and red. Certain coaches are named.

Regn. Number	Chassis Make and Type	Body Make and Seats	Date New	Notes
LXR 958	Van Hool 'Astromega' TD824	Van Hool CH53/22CT	1983	(a)
MLK 418L	Daimler 'Fleetline' CRG6LX	Park Royal H44/27D	1972	(b)
KJD 218P	Scania Metropolitan BR111DH	Metro-Cammell H43/29D	1976	(c)
KJD 241P	"	"	"	(c)
NVD 328P	Leyland 'Leopard' PSU3C/4R	Duple C36F	"	
OUC 111R	Scania Metropolitan BR111DH	Metro-Cammell H43/29D	"	(c)
UAV 965S	Leyland 'Leopard' PSU3E/4R	Plaxton C53F	1978	(d)
UAV 966S	"	"	"	(d)
KAD 349V	Leyland 'Leopard' PSU5C/4R	Plaxton C57F	1980	(e)
KAD 350V	"	"	"	(e)
FNM 858Y	Leyland 'Tiger' TRCTL11/3R	Plaxton C48FT	1983	(f)
KBM 533Y	Leyland 'Tiger' TRCTL11/2R	Plaxton C50F	"	
C411 HHL	Leyland 'Royal Tiger'	Leyland C49FT	1985	(g)

NOTES:-
(a) LXR 958 was ex Park, Hamilton in 1985; it was originally registered MSU 586Y, and was re-registered by Park's in 1983
(b) MLK 418L was ex London Transport No. DMS418 in 1979
(c) KJD 218/241P, OUC 111R were ex London Transport Nos. MD18/41/111 in 1984
(d) UAV 965/966S were ex Whippet, Fenstanton, in 1981
(e) KAD 349/350V were ex National Travel (South-West) Nos. 349/350 in 1984

(f) FNM 858Y was ex Ebdon, Sidcup, in 1984
(g) C411 HHL was delivered registered C945 LRT, and was exhibited at the 1985 Motor Show, London, bearing the latter number before being re-registered

Crystals Coaches

Mr C J Springham commenced to trade as 'Crystal Cars' at 10 Station Road, Sidcup, in January 1972. By 1973 the fleet totalled four minibuses. In December 1975 the address was changed to 5 Norman Parade, Maylands Drive, Sidcup. A further move took place to the present address, Bridge Road, Orpington, in July 1978.

Miss J Normington's 'Orpington & District' firm withdrew service 858 (Orpington - Biggin Hill) in January 1981, and the rolling stock was disposed of. This route, which needs small vehicles, was taken over by Crystals, which by now owned one of the largest fleets of PSV minibuses in Britain. The 858 is worked with one bus shuttling up and down (the service frequency is every 70-75 minutes throughout the day), but it forms only a small part of the firm's activities. On August 10th 1985 Crystals took over operation of London Regional Transport service 146 (Bromley North Station to Downe via Keston), using Leyland 'Cub' midibuses.

Regn. Number	Chassis Make and Type	Body Make and Seats	Date New	Notes
OCJ 960M	Bedford CFS	Dormobile 12-seat	1974	(a)
HYK 514N	Ford 'Transit'	"	1975	(b)
JAW 687N	Bedford CFS	"	1974	(c)
LGW 995P	"	Dormobile 11-seat	1975	(c)
MPW 171P	"	Dormobile 12-seat	1976	(d)
NGW 793P	Leyland 'Sherpa' 240	Williams 12-seat	"	
NGW 794P	"	"	"	
OMY 124R	"	"	"	
OMY 126R	"	"	"	
OVJ 21R	Bedford CFS	Dormobile 12-seat	"	(c)
PFO 216R	"	"	"	(c)
PVS 558R	Ford 'Transit'	Dormobile B16F	"	(e)
RGX 324R	"	? 12-seat	1977	
RMY 758R	"	Dormobile 12-seat	"	
RMY 759R	"	"	"	
RJU 399R	"	"	1976	(f)
TYB 128R	"	"	1977	(g)
THE 933S	Volkswagen LT28	Williams 12-seat	"	(h)
UFG 145S	Bedford YMT	Duple C53F	"	(i)
VNK 595S	Ford 'Transit'	Dormobile B16F	"	
VNK 599S	"	Tricentrol 12-seat	1978	(j)
WGU 104S	"	Dormobile 12-seat	"	
WNH 241S	"	Dormobile B16F	"	(k)
WVV 4S	"	"	"	(l)
XYA 516S	Bedford CFS	Dormobile 12-seat	1977	(m)
BPV 576T	Bedford CFL	Reeves Burgess C17F	1978	(n)
EYC 623T	Bedford CFS	Dormobile 12-seat	"	(o)
HYC 33T	"	"	1979	(p)
FNB 277V	Mercedes-Benz L508DG	Deansgate C21F	"	(q)
MSU 434V	Volkswagen LT28	Devon 12-seat	1980	(r)

Regn. Number	Chassis Make and Type	Body Make and Seats	Date New	Notes
WNP 514V	Volkswagen LT28	Devon 12-seat	1980	(s)
NRM 600W	Mercedes-Benz L608D	Reeves Burgess C25F	1981	(t)
TLC 73W	Volkswagen LT28	Devon 12-seat	"	(u)
HCR 688X	Fiat 35F8	Robin Hood 12-seat	1982	(v)
LFR 301X	"	Harwin 12-seat	"	(w)
OWJ 460X	Leyland 'Cub'	Reeves Burgess B33F	1981	(x)
RCP 30CX	Mercedes-Benz L508D	? C15F	"	(y)
ULD 568X	Volkswagen LT28	Devon 12-seat	"	(u)
VNA 726X	Ford 'Transit'	Williams 12-seat	1982	(z)
FBM 924Y	"	Trimoco 12-seat	"	(aa)
XHD 345Y	Mercedes-Benz L307D	Whittaker C12F	"	(ab)
A691 DMV	Leyland 'Cub'	Reeves Burgess C25F	1983	
A390 SGB	Mercedes-Benz L307D	Whittaker 12-seat	"	(ac)
A525 TGB	"	"	"	(ac)
A382 XMC	Ford 'Transit'	Dormobile B16F	1982	(z)
B489 CHE	Fiat 35F9	Coachcraft 12-seat	1984	
B490 CHE	"	"	"	
B499 CHE	"	"	"	
B811 EHE	"	"	1985	
B812 EHE	"	"	"	
B820 EHE	"	Coachcraft C14F	"	
B434 FJX	Fiat 79F14	Coachcraft C19F	1984	
B279 KGW	Mercedes-Benz 210D	Coachcraft 12-seat	"	
B401 KGY	Mercedes-Benz L210D	"	"	
B867 NMX	Ford 'Transit'	Mellor C16F	1985	
C374 BKJ	"	Dormobile C16F	"	
C763 EPP	"	Trimoco 12-seat	"	
C671 RMX	Mercedes-Benz 608D	Mercedes/Rootes B19F	"	

NOTES:-
(a) OCJ 960M was ex Gclynia, Long Melford, in 1982
(b) HYK 514N was acquired from an unknown owner in 1980
(c) JAW 687N, LGW 995P, OVJ 21R and PFO 216R were ex Everest, Swanley, in 1979
(d) MPW 171P was ex Ward, Mundesley, in 1980
(e) PVS 558R was ex Reading Minibus Hire, Caversham, in 1981
(f) RJU 399R was ex Cleverly, Pontypool, in 1979
(g) TYB 128R was ex Lynch, Ware, in 1984
(h) THE 933S was ex Dennett, Yeovil, in 1982
(i) UFG 145S was ex Stanbridge, Turners Hill, in 1981
(j) VNK 599S was ex Whyman, London NW1, in 1978
(k) WNH 241S was ex Johnson, Stanford, No. 9 in 1982
(l) WVV 4S was ex Country Lion, Northampton, in 1981
(m) XYA 516S was ex Moger, Conford, in 1983
(n) BPV 576T was ex Blue & White, London W1, in 1983
(o) EYC 623T was ex Telling, Byfleet, in 1982
(p) HYC 33T was ex Thamesmead, London SE18, in 1982
(q) FNB 277V was ex Newsome, Barnsley, in 1982
(r) MSU 434V was formerly registered MGE 932V and was previously operated by Swan National, London W4 as a non-PSV
(s) WNP 514V was ex Patterson, Birmingham, in 1984
(t) NRM 600W was ex Irving, Dalston, in 1983
(u) TLC 73W and ULD 568X were ex Swan National, London W4, in 1983
(v) HCR 688X was ex Barfoot, West End, in 1985
(w) LFR 301X was acquired from a private owner in 1984
(x) OWJ 460X was ex Kenning's Motorway Services, Sheffield (non-PSV) in 1985
(y) RCP 300X was ex Jowitt, Tankersley, in 1984
(z) VNA 726X and A382 XMC were acquired from unknown owners in 1985
(aa) FBM 924Y was ex Lunar Module, Luton, in 1984
(ab) XHD 345Y was ex Brown, South Kirkby, in 1985

(ac) A390 SGB and A525 TGB were ex Albany, Glasgow, in 1985

J R Dell—
Rover Bus Service

During the 1920s Mr H Dunham, formerly a driver for the 'General', founded the 'Gleaner' bus undertaking in Chesham - using an anagram of his former employer's fleetname. Doubtless he was a successful gleaner, for he attracted the notice of larger competitors, and was taken over by Messrs Clarke of Chesham ('Chesham & District'). They were in turn acquired by Amersham & District, one of the larger independent firms taken over by the LPTB in 1933.

Mr J R G Dell, one of Mr Dunham's drivers, rather than join the big company with his boss, founded his own firm in 1928. Since then his 'Rover Bus Service' has prospered, with two basic stage services running between Chesham and Hemel Hempstead - one via Flaunden and the other via Whelpley Hill, both operating daily except Sundays. At peak periods, one journey in each direction is extended to operate beyond Chesham to and from Amersham. Until 1964 the Chesham - Hemel Hempstead run was operated jointly with London Transport (route 316), one of the very few examples of joint operation between LT or London Country and an independent.

For most of the history of Rover Bus Service, the late Mr J R G Dell was in sole charge; his son, Mr J R Dell, became proprietor in October 1977 after a brief period in partnership with his father. Mr Dell senior died in April 1978, after a half-century's service to the local population's public transport needs.

The early days of Rover Bus Service saw an assortment of buses and coaches of Chevrolet, AJS, Dennis, Gilford and Commer manufacture. For a long time now, however, lightweight Bedfords and Fords have predominated, but recently two Leyland 'Tigers' and a Mercedes-Benz have been acquired. The head office and garage are at Delmar, Lycrome Road, Lye Green. Fleet livery is light blue and cream.

Regn. Number	Chassis Make and Type	Body Make and Seats	Date New	Notes
OJR 338	Bedford YLQ	Duple B45F	1978	(a)
JEV 474N	Ford R1014	Willowbrook B43F	1975	(b)
LHW 508P	Bedford YMT	Plaxton C53F	1976	(c)
OVV 53R	Ford R1014	Duple B43F	"	(d)
SBH 103R	Bedford YMT	Plaxton C53F	1977	(e)
VVD 434S	"	Duple C53F	"	(f)
FBM 425T	"	Plaxton C53F	1978	
KBH 862V	"	Duple C53F	1979	
PNM 663W	Ford R1114	Duple B55F	1980	(g)
SNM 441W	Bedford YNT	Duple C53F	"	(h)
BFP 261Y	Leyland 'Tiger' TRCTL11/3R	Plaxton C57F	1981	
HBH 423Y	Bedford YNT	Plaxton C53F	1983	(i)
A148 RMJ	Leyland 'Tiger' TRCTL11/3R	Plaxton C55F	"	(j)
B265 AMG	Mercedes-Benz L608D	Reeves Burgess C19F	1984	

NOTES:-
(a) OJR 338 was re-registered ex YBH 368S in 1985
(b) JEV 474N was ex Ford Motor Co, Warley, in 1979
(c) LHW 508P was ex Morley, West Row, in 1985
(d) OVV 53R was ex United Counties Omnibus Co No. 53 in 1982
(e) SBH 103R was ex Plaskow & Margo, London W3, in 1978
(f) VVD 434S was ex Panatlas, London W3, in 1980

(g) KBH 862V was ex Armchair, Brentford, in 1982
(h) PNM 663W was ex Eyres-Scott (Lee-Roy), Brentwood in 1984
(i) HBH 423Y was ex Armchair, Brentford, in 1984
(j) A148 RMJ was ex Cavalier, Hounslow in 1985

Golden Boy Coaches (Jetsie Ltd)

Mr W J McIntyre founded Golden Boy Coaches at Woodcroft, Harlow, in August 1968. Two of the first vehicles owned were Bristol KSW double-deckers from Wilts & Dorset, for contract work. Ever since then, the firm has maintained a double-deck contract fleet; Bristol 'Lodekkas' have figured prominently most of the time, but more exotic vehicles have included Leyland 'Tigers' rebuilt to double-deck by Barton, an AEC rebuilt by Hanson's of Huddersfield, and several ex-Aldershot & District Dennis 'Lolines'. The present double-deck fleet is a pair of AEC 'Regent' Mk Vs from East Kent.

In 1971 Golden Boy moved to Low Hill Garage, Roydon, where it remained for twelve years. It was at the Roydon address that the firm first became a limited company, Golden Boy Coaches Ltd., in December 1974; by then the fleet contained 7 coaches and 4 double-deckers. The custom of giving the newer coaches girls' names started in 1972 and continues to the present day. During the Roydon period another member of the family, Mr J T McIntyre, operated a small fleet trading as Maxi Coach Hire; this was extant for two distinct periods, from 1976 to 1978 and from 1979 to 1981.

In 1983 Golden Boy Coaches moved to the present address at 1 Amwell Street, Hoddesdon, and in May 1985 the business was formed into a new company, Jetsie Ltd. In September 1985 Golden Boy Coaches tendered successfully to take over services 392/393 and 501 from London Country. London Country still works the 501, as a shopping service three days a week from Ongar to Romford; the Harlow - Ongar section of the 501 has been joined to the 392 service to create an hourly through route from Hoddesdon to Ongar. The 393 continues to operate on its own from Hoddesdon to Harlow. Regular vehicles on the 392 service are a batch of Bristol LHs with Plaxton coach bodies which came secondhand from Devon General. The network normally requires four single-deck vehicles to operate it throughout the day.

Regn. Number	Chassis Make and Type	Body Make and Seats	Date New	Notes
GJG 737D	AEC 'Regent' Mk V 2D3RA	Park Royal H40/32F	1966	(a)
GJG 740D	"	"	"	(a)
HVD 744N	Bedford YRT	Plaxton C53F	1975	(b)
JPC 834N	"	"	"	(b)
JHW 124P	Bristol LH6L	ECW B43F	"	(c)
OKY 84R	Leyland 'Leopard' PSU5B/4R	Plaxton C55F	1977	(d)
SFJ 116R	Bristol LH6L	Plaxton C41F	"	(e)
SFJ 117R	"	"	"	(e)
SFJ 120R	"	"	"	(e)
SFJ 122R	"	"	"	(e)
JMJ 113V	Ford/Tricentrol R1014	Plaxton C35F	1979	(f)
KRO 645V	Ford R1114	Duple C53F	1980	(g)
KRO 646V	"	"	"	(g)
DNK 580Y	Mercedes-Benz L508D	Reeves Burgess C19F	1982	
DNK 581Y	Leyland 'Tiger' TRCTL11/3R	Plaxton C50F	"	(h)
DNK 582Y	Bedford YNT	Plaxton C53F	"	(h)

NOTES:-
(a) GJG 737/740D were ex East Kent Road Car Co Ltd Nos. 7737/7740 in 1982
(b) HVD 744N and JPC 834N were ex Rickards, Brentford, in 1982
(c) JHW 124P was ex Bristol Omnibus Co Ltd No. 364 in 1984
(d) OKY 84R was ex National Travel East Ltd in 1982, and is named "Miss Kathy"
(e) SFJ 116/117/120/122R were ex Devon General Ltd Nos. 3116/3117/3120/3122 in 1985
(f) The chassis of JMJ 113V was shortened by Tricentrol Chassis Developments before bodying
(g) KRO 645/646V exchanged identities with each other in 1983; they are named "Miss Bernadette" and "Miss Jacqueline" respectively
(h) DNK 581/582Y are named "Miss Mary" and "Miss Angela" respectively

Guards (Inter—City) Ltd

Mr R P J Churchman founded the enterprise later to be known as Guards Coaches in February 1965, by buying a Commer 'Avenger' from Austin's of Stafford. A few months later this vehicle was joined by a Ford/Duple coach. These two vehicles passed to a new limited company, Guards Coaches Ltd, incorporated in May 1966; the name was no doubt inspired by the nearby Guards Depot, a military establishment which had been part of the local scenery of Caterham for many years. The company's name was later changed to the present title, Guards (Inter-City) Ltd. At about the end of 1969, the address was moved to 103 Croydon Road, Caterham. In August 1974 there was a further move, to 78 Spencer Road, Caterham, and in March 1976 yet another move took the company to 26 Station Avenue, Caterham.

In the meantime Mr Churchman had helped to found the much larger company, Guards Coaches (London) Ltd in 1970, which explains why both companies used similar blue and white liveries and almost identical fleetnames. Mr Churchman sold his controlling share of the London company in 1974, since when there has been no direct link between the two companies.

Guards of Caterham operates the Coulsdon - Clock House Estate (The Mount) stage service. This has had an eventful history; it was pioneered by London Transport as Saturdays-only route 263, and passed to Banstead Coaches in 1964. They continued it until June 1980, when it was taken over by Tandridge Taxis Ltd of Coulsdon, who used a secondhand Dodge 12-seater minibus on it. In May 1982 Tandridge Taxis ceased trading and the route (but not the vehicle) passed to Guards. The usual vehicle for this route is the Ford 20-seat midibus. The service runs on Mondays to Fridays only, with a 30-minute frequency observed for most of the day. In 1985 a route change, the first since Banstead Coaches had taken the route over, was made to extend the area served.

Regn. Number	Chassis Make and Type	Body Make and Seats	Date New	Notes
TNB 442K	Bedford VAS5	Duple C29F	1972	(a)
CFX 948T	Ford 'Transit'	Bristol Street 12-seat	1979	
PRO 449W	Mercedes-Benz 508D	Reeves Burgess C21F	1980	
FNM 740Y	Ford A0610	Mellor B20F	1983	(b)
(Ordered)	Mercedes-Benz	Reeves Burgess C21F	----	
(Ordered)	"	Reeves Burgess 12-seat	----	

NOTES:-
(a) TNB 442K was ex Tuck, Chaldon, in 1984

All photographs in this book are by A M WITTON

In this area the Bristol LH is a more commonly seen vehicle in the fleets of independent companies than with London Country! A major user of the type is Blue Saloon of Guildford whose KPB 881P, one of three LHs bought new and several second-hand ones, was photographed in Guildford's Friary Bus Station.

The Banstead Coaches fleet has long contained one service bus amongst all the coaches, for the Banstead - Chipstead Valley service. GPA 846N, the current example, was bought second-hand from Tillingbourne and is seen against a backdrop of mock-Tudor shopping parades in the centre of its new home town.

In contrast, Biss Bros, which once ran double-deckers on its bus routes, is now content to allocate an ordinary Bedford/Plaxton coach to this duty. JVS 935N is in the new bus station in Bishops Stortford which replaces a large number of on-street stopping places.

17

Characteristic of the British Airways 'airside bus' fleet at Heathrow Airport are a number of unusual-looking Leyland Nationals with **three** entrance doors! Showing its third (i.e. offside) door to the camera is BU280 (NLP 389V), still wearing the old-style British Airways livery and fleetname.

Cook's of Biggleswade runs three Scania 'Metropolitans' bought from London Transport, as well as one surviving DMS-type 'Fleetline' from the same stable. Scania KJD 241P, fitted with a destination blind for the Stevenage service, is sandwiched between the Fleetline and an ex-National Travel 'Leopard' in this view taken at Biggleswade garage.

Many operators apply "cherished" registrations to their newer coaches, but that idea was not good enough for Dell's of Chesham! Their only re-registered vehicle, OJR 338, is a 1978-vintage Bedford/Duple bus. It was seen on service at Lye Green, outside Dell's garage.

Golden Boy Coaches of Hoddesdon are relative newcomers to stage operation; their working of the Hoddesdon - Harlow - Ongar routes is barely four months old as we go to press. Regulars on these duties are four Bristol LHs with Plaxton coach bodies, bought from Devon General, whose fleetnumber plate still adorns SFJ 116R in this Harlow Bus Station view.

RWC 651W is not only the last Bedford in stock with Frank Harris Coaches, but also by far the smallest coach in the fleet. At this angle, however, shown between two older coaches now withdrawn, it looks almost the same size as its bigger sisters. The now-vacated coach park at appropriately-named Parker Road, Grays, was the venue.

London Country's small contribution to the Bristol LH tally is a total of five survivors of the BN class, with 7'6" wide ECW bodies designed for "tight squeeze" routes. BN59 (TPJ 59S) was seen in Chesham Broadway wearing Chilternlink "local identity" fleetnames.

ECW bodywork has never been particularly common with London Country or its predecessors (though see page 40!), but by coincidence our three LCBS illustrations are all of ECW-bodied vehicles. LRC7 (B107 LPH), one of a fleet of ten Leyland 'Olympians' with ECW coach bodies, is seen parked in Luton bus station wearing the current "stripey" Green Line livery.

Green Lines and airports are good neighbours; London's airports at Heathrow, Gatwick, Luton and more recently Stansted, are important pivots of the Green Line network. TL1 (TPC 101X), first of a fleet of 42 ECW-bodied Leyland "Tigers", sails down Park Lane, London as it approaches journey's end on the non-stop run from Luton Airport to Victoria.

Moore's Imperial buses are an inseparable part of the scenery in the very imperial town of Windsor. These two Ford/Plaxton buses bought from Midland Red in 1978 are still going strong with the Windsor firm. YHA 314J awaits departure from the Theatre Royal terminus, showing a route board for the direct Castle - Ruddlesway route.

(b) FNM 740Y was ex Ash (Mole Valley), Leatherhead, in 1985

Frank Harris (Coaches) Ltd

Mr F R Harris founded this coach business in 1923; his family had been involved in horse-drawn road haulage back into the late 19th century. The first coach was a Palladium charabanc named 'Mons Angel'. From about 1927 the firm ran a workmen's service between Grays and Purfleet, and a dockworkers' service from Grays to the Royal Albert Dock in east London. However, these services were lost to London Transport on 17th May 1934. Two vehicles, a Leyland 20-seater and a Commer 'Invader' 19-seater, were also transferred to the LPTB, but the bulk of the fleet was retained by Mr Harris. Road haulage activities were also developed and remained under the same management as the coaches until nationalisation of road haulage in 1948; the lorries were later bought back by the family and in 1958 two limited companies were created, Frank Harris (Coaches) Ltd taking the passenger-carrying business and Harris Haulage (Grays) Ltd inheriting the lorries.

The bus services were a fairly minor activity, and their loss proved no constraint to the management. Summer coach services were started from the Grays area to many coastal resorts, and Harris's dark green and grey coaches became a familiar sight far from their home. Harrington coachwork was standardised for many years, but the last example of this handsome make of bodywork in the fleet was withdrawn several years ago.

Continental express services were started in 1980 when Harris (along with Grey-Green Coaches) took over National Travel's interest in the London – Munich route. The three partners on this route are now Harris, L'Epervier of Belgium and Deutsche Touring of Germany; coaches run daily in the summer. In 1984 the Transline pool was started, for express services to Germany from various points in the UK. Harris also operates "shuttle" coach services in the summer months to Cap d'Agde and to the Taize religious community, both in France.

The head office and garage was at the Harris family home in Parker Road, Grays, from the early days of the haulage business. In April 1984 the company moved to Manor Road, West Thurrock. There is also an outstation at Corringham. Fleet livery is the traditional green and grey.

Regn. Number	Chassis Make and Type	Body Make and Seats	Date New	Notes
2396 FH	Volvo B58-61	Plaxton C53F	1977	(a)
2942 FH	Bova 'Futura' FLD12-280	Bova C53F	1984	(b)
6330 FH	Volvo B58-61	Plaxton C53F	1977	(a)
NOV 804G	Daimler 'Fleetline' CRG6LX	Park Royal H43/29D	1968	(c)
JGU 287K	Daimler 'Fleetline' CRG6LXB	Metro-Cammell H44/27F	1972	(d)
MLH 318L	"	"	"	(d)
MLH 358L	"	"	1973	(d)
MLH 361L	"	"	"	(d)
NEV 104P	Volvo B58-56	Plaxton C44F	1976	
XVW 450S	DAF MB200DKL550	"	1978	
XVW 452S	DAF MB200DKL600	Plaxton C53F	"	
XVW 453S	"	"	"	
FTW 131T	"	"	1979	
FTW 132T	"	"	"	

Regn. Number	Chassis Make and Type	Body Make and Seats	Date New	Notes
NEV 770V	DAF MB200DKTL600	Plaxton C50F	1980	
NEV 772V	"	Plaxton C53F	"	
NEV 773V	"	"	"	
NEV 774V	DAF MB200DKTL550	Plaxton C49F	"	
RWC 651W	Bedford/Tricentrol YMQ/S	Plaxton C30F	"	
UHK 201W	DAF MB200DKTL600	Plaxton C50F	1981	
UHK 202W	"	"	"	
UHK 203W	DAF SB2005DHU	Plaxton C46F	"	
WHK 81W	Bova EL26/581	Bova C50F	"	
AOO 101X	"	"	1982	
AOC 102X	"	"	"	
CGP 311X	"	Bova C46FT	1981	(e)
FHJ 83Y	DAF MB200DKFL	Van Hool C48FT	1983	
FHJ 84Y	"	"	"	
A86 RWC	Bova 'Futura' FHD12-280	Bova C53F	1984	
A698 TNO	"	Bova C48FT	"	
B87 CEV	"	"	1985	
B88 CEV	"	"	"	
B89 CNO	Van Hool T815	Van Hool C48FT	"	

NOTES:-
(a) 2396/6330 FH were re-registered ex TVW 21/22R in 1984
(b) 2942 FH was re-registered ex A953 TJN in 1984
(c) NOV 804G was ex West Midlands PTE No. 3804 in 1983
(d) JGU 287K, MLH 318/358/361L were ex West Midlands PTE Nos. 5520/5540/5570/5572 in 1985
(e) CGP 311X was ex Michaels, Carshalton, No. 59 in 1982

Lee—Roy Coaches

Mr R Eyres-Scott was running a coach business in Brentwood by 1960, and in March 1972 he started trading as Lee-Roy Coaches from an address in nearby Hutton. His initial rolling stock consisted of a Bedford SB3 and a Ford coach, together with a Ford 'Transit' minibus, acquired from Dover of Brentwood. Ever since then, Fords have formed an important part of the Lee-Roy fleet.

In February 1976 the business, by now owning four vehicles including a double-decker, passed to a partnership of Messrs R & C Eyres-Scott. In October 1978 the firm moved to the present address at Ongar Road, Kelvedon Hatch, near Brentwood.

In May 1982 Lee-Roy Coaches took over most of the activities of G F Ward Ltd of Epping. Ward's had been started in 1953 by Mr G F Ward at Fairfield Road, Epping, with an Austin 29-seater coach which remained the only vehicle for four and a half years. The business was incorporated as a Limited Company in 1973, and moved to Bower Hill, Epping, in 1979. Lee-Roy Coaches acquired several coaches, the Epping depot, and bus route 381 which Ward's had taken over from London Country Bus Services on August 9th 1971. This route runs between Broadley Common and Toothill via Epping, and had been extended to serve Blake Hall and Bobbingworth. Under Lee-Roy management the timetable for this service consists of a basic Monday to Friday run from Coopersale Common to Epping Green, with extensions to Broadley Common (schooldays), Toothill and Greenstead Green (Mondays and Fridays) and Leaside Nursery and Lower Nazeing (Mondays). The operation of this route and other Epping area activities continue to be based at Ward's former Epping garage.

Regn. Number	Chassis Make and Type	Body Make and Seats	Date New	Notes
4849 RU	MAN SR280	MAN C28F	1980	(a)
TDL 569K	Bristol RELL6G	ECW B53F	1972	(b)
MRU 68P	Ford R1014	Plaxton C41F	1976	(d)
OKY 63R	AEC 'Reliance' 6U3ZR	Plaxton C55F	1977	(e)
EUE 337T	Ford R1114	Plaxton C53F	1979	(f)
EUE 338T	"	"	"	(f)
NFJ 368W	Mercedes-Benz 0303/15R	Jonckheere C48FT	1981	(g)
JVW 158Y	Volvo B10M-61	Berkhof C49FT	1983	
A117 SNH	Mercedes-Benz 0303/15R	Jonckheere C38FT	1984	(a)

NOTES:-
(a) 4849 RU and A117 SNH were ex South Eastern, Hornchurch, in 1985; 4849 RU was previously registered GMC 569V
(b) TDL 569K was ex Southern Vectis Omnibus Co No. 869 in 1983
(c) TMT 438M was ex Blue Line, Upminster, in 1975
(d) MRU 68P was ex Continental Coach, London SW5, in 1980
(e) OKY 63R was ex Viking Safaris, London WC2, in 1983
(f) EUE 337/338T were ex Ward, Epping, in 1982
(g) NFJ 368W was ex Trathen, Roborough, in 1984

London Country Bus Services Ltd

London Country Bus Services dates back only to 1970, but its Reigate headquarters are on the site of the head office of the East Surrey Traction Co Ltd, founded in 1911. After two other attempts to link Reigate and Redhill with a motorbus service, East Surrey's founder, Arthur Hawkins, made the third and successful attempt. He had written anonymously to 'Motor Traction' magazine asking about the economics of a bus service over this distance. He received an encouraging reply which led to the formation of the company. East Surrey's services rapidly spread in all directions from its Reigate base, though staying generally to the south of the River Thames and well outside the LGOC's London territory.

The National Omnibus & Transport Co set up bases in London's northern outskirts in 1919, after earlier operating Clarkson steam buses on the streets of London itself. National was also the parent of Eastern National, Southern National and Western National, which became completely separate in 1929.

In view of the need for good relations with its northern and southern neighbours, in 1921 the LGOC signed an operating agreement with East Surrey, whereby the former undertook to equip the East Surrey fleet, and the latter would work an expanded route network on the General's behalf. East Surrey remained independent, but came to rely on LGOC standard vehicle types, mainly of ADC and AEC manufacture - although a few non-standard buses were also bought, mainly for low-density rural services for which General had no suitable buses. A 1928 Act of Parliament gave the four main-line railways powers to operate bus services, and to forestall the danger that the Southern Railway would make a takeover bid for East Surrey, the LGCC bought East Surrey outright in 1929.

North of London, the LGOC made another agreement with the National company, also in 1921, whereby the latter would work services on LGOC's behalf; here again, quantities of LGOC standard buses were put into the National garages concerned, which began to stand apart from National's provincial bus interests. Finally in 1932, the LGOC merged East Surrey with another subsidiary bought in 1929 (Amersham & District) and with its National interests, into a new company - London General Country Services Ltd., with headquarters at Reigate. LGCS remained intact for only a year (1932/1933), after which its operations and those of many independents were taken into the LPTB's Country Area.

Although the General controlled its own services in inner London, and those of the associated companies in the outer areas, there was much competition on the lucrative express coach services from the suburbs to the City and West End. Due to a loophole in the law, such coach services were exempt from some of the rules for buses 'plying for hire' in the Metropolitan Police Area. The General decided to try for a share of this market. In 1929 a fleet of AEC coaches went into service on a Watford - London express route under the 'General' name; in the following year the East Surrey company and Autocar Ltd of Tunbridge Wells joined the operation. Later in 1930 the General created a subsidiary, Green Line Coaches Ltd, to acquire its coaching business and those of East Surrey and Autocar. The new company expanded, partly at the expense of smaller firms, and linked its routes across London, with a central coach station situated at first at Poland Street, Oxford Circus. Thus a comprehensive Green Line network was handed over to the LPTB in 1933. The coaches originally carried a system of route letters, some with number suffixes; the present numbers in the 700 series did not begin until 1946, and many of the present services are more recent still.

Since 1970 London Country has reshaped the Green Line network drastically; many of the London radial services have been abolished or reduced, and none are now linked across London. However, extensive new services has been created, many of them focussed on London's airports at Heathrow, Gatwick and Luton. Most recently Green Line coaches have begun to break out of the traditional London Country area; joint services have been started between London and Oxford (shared with City of Oxford) and between London and Cambridge (shared with Eastern Counties, later Cambus). Green Line coaches are also seen much further afield - as far as Aberdeen for example! - now that they share the working of several National Express services.

In 1933 London General Country Services Ltd was transferred to the LPTB and became the nucleus of the Board's Country Area. Although the Country Area's vehicles carried 'London Transport' fleetnames, they were painted green instead of red, and the Country Area was regarded as a partly independent unit run from its Reigate headquarters. Standard LPTB buses arrived with a few modifications; for example the 12 'Godstone STLs', AEC 'Regents' with Weymann lowbridge forward-entrance bodies, ordered by LGCS but delivered to LPTB, were followed by large batches of forward-entrance STLs built to LPTB design, all for the Country Area. The logic was that with a forward entrance it was easier for the driver to line up the platform with the many tiny bus stops tucked into hedgerows. The 10T10 class (AEC 'Regals') and several other Green Line types were delivered to replace the original Green Line fleet; several of the original Green Line coaches were rebodied as buses. Postwar, almost the only difference between the Central and Country Areas was the difference in livery; especially with the RTs and RFs, vehicles often changed livery from red to green or vice versa during their lives. It was not unknown for red buses to be lent to Country Area garages, for example at Bank Holiday weekends, to release green buses to work as Green Line reliefs. Country Area services were numbered in separate blocks of the LT number series; those north of the Thames became 300-399 with an overflow series from 800 upwards, while those south of the river were 400-499 and 851 upwards. Although LCBS is now a completely separate company, the LT-inspired service numbers continue to be used - with a few 'oddities' such as services operated jointly with NBC neighbours. The 300 and 400 series were laid down for services entering the Metropolitan Police Area as long ago as 1924, at the instigation of the Metropolitan Police, which numbered all London's bus services at that time.

The Country Area passed to the London Transport Executive in 1948 and to the London Transport Board in 1963. For a time in the late 1950s, London Transport's splendid collection of preserved buses and trams was stored at Reigate garage.

In 1969 the Government proposed to transfer control of LT to the Greater London Council. The GLC did not want to look after services as far afield as Guildford, Tunbridge Wells, Bishop's Stortford, Luton and Windsor, in some cases 15 miles beyond the GLC boundary. Accordingly the Country Area was formed into a new company, London Country Bus Services Ltd., again with headquarters at Reigate; LCBS's ring-shaped operating territory is really a result of the LGOC's manoeuvres of the 1920s. LCBS is a subsidiary of the NBC, and since its establishment new vehicle types have been of typical NBC designs such as the Leyland 'Atlantean' and 'Olympian', the National, the Bristol LH and a few Bristol VRs which were later sold to the Bristol Omnibus Co. It was decided to lease rather than purchase most of the 'Green Line' and private-hire coach fleet, replacing them over a fairly short life so that this front-line fleet could be kept up-to-date. AEC 'Reliances' were delivered from 1977 onwards, but all have now been replaced by Leyland 'Leopards' and 'Tigers'. The latter model has become the Green Line standard, after a brief trial of the Volvo B58 as a possible replacement for the 'Reliance'. The vast fleet of LT-type vehicles, including 'Routemasters', 'Merlins', 'Swifts' and even some elderly RTs and RFs, gave way to the new vehicles, and apart from a handful of officially preserved vehicles the influence of LT on London Country's fleet has now disappeared. Most of the 'Routemasters' were sold back to London Transport, where some re-entered service as red London buses; others have been used as training buses or broken up for spare parts.

In 1980 the 50th anniversary of the Green Line coach network was celebrated with rallies and other special events. Several Green Line coaches were repainted in a special 'Golden Jubilee' livery with a broad gold band. A range of older Green Line coaches, from the London Transport Collection and other sources, was assembled to show the development of the breed from the assorted machines which started the Green Line system in 1930.

From May 1984 National Travel (London) Ltd, the inheritor of the London-based coaching operations once run under the Timpson, Tilling and Samuelson names, was placed under London Country's operational control. National Travel (London) Ltd however retains a separate operator's licence and (of course) its own premises and vehicles, so as long as this situation continues it will be treated as a coach company in its own right in future editions of 'Fleetbook 15 - Buses of Inner London'. There is also London Crusader Ltd, an NBC-owned marketing company which finds customers for NBC operators in the London area. LCBS's open-top 'Atlanteans' which are used on the Round London Sightseeing Tour are run under London Crusader auspices, but London Crusader actually owns no vehicles and therefore cannot be treated as a separate operator.

When first established, LCBS adopted LT Country Area's dark green and cream livery, but used a 'winged wheel' emblem in place of the LT 'bullseye'. Later, a Lincoln green and yellow livery was applied. Now NBC leaf green livery is applied; the 'local coach' livery of leaf green and white was applied to some dual-purpose Nationals for Green Line work, but most were later repainted into bus livery, and Green Line and private-hire coaches were given a livery of white with a broad green waistband carrying the Green Line name and NBC logo. Recently, coaches have appeared in a Green Line version of the 'stripey' livery now fashionable for NBC coach fleets, and the latest bus livery is an attractive combination of leaf green with light green waistbands and fleetnames.

Garage codes are shown in white paint on the offside and nearside waistlines, accompanied by a 'running number'. The newest coaches, however, display their garage codes in one of the licence disc holders, and the 'running number' is shown in a bracket inside the windscreen. Garages are known by the following codes:-

CM - Chelsham	GY - Grays	RG - Reigate
CY - Crawley	HA - Harlow	SA - St Albans
DG - Dunton Green	HF - Hatfield	SJ - Swanley
DS - Dorking	HG - Hertford	(to close in early 1986)
DT - Dartford	HH - Hemel Hempstead	SL - Slough
GD - Godstone	LH - Leatherhead	ST - Staines
GF - Guildford	MA - Amersham	SV - Stevenage
GR - Watford (Garston)	NF - Northfleet	WY - Addlestone

The Central Works is at Tinsley Green, Crawley New Town; there is a Northern Works at Garston. The Head Office occupies a large site adjacent to Reigate Garage, at the corner of Bell Street and Lesbourne Road, Reigate.

AN5-120

Chassis: Leyland 'Atlantean' PDR1A/1 Special, built 1972
Body: (AN11-90) Park Royal H43/29D
(AN91-105/107-109/111-120) Metro-Cammell H43/29D
(AN5/10/106/110) Metro-Cammell O43/29D

AN5	JPL 105K	AN38	JPL 138K	AN65	JPL 165K	AN92	MPJ 192L
AN10	JPL 110K	AN39	JPL 139K	AN66	JPL 166K	AN93	MPJ 193L
AN11	JPL 111K	AN40	JPL 140K	AN67	JPL 167K	AN94	MPJ 194L
AN12	JPL 112K	AN41	JPL 141K	AN68	JPL 168K	AN95	MPJ 195L
AN13	JPL 113K	AN42	JPL 142K	AN69	JPL 169K	AN96	MPJ 196L
AN15	JPL 115K	AN43	JPL 143K	AN70	JPL 170K	AN97	MPJ 197L
AN16	JPL 116K	AN44	JPL 144K	AN71	JPL 171K	AN100	MPJ 200L
AN17	JPL 117K	AN45	JPL 145K	AN72	JPL 172K	AN101	MPJ 201L
AN18	JPL 118K	AN46	JPL 146K	AN73	JPL 173K	AN102	MPJ 202L
AN19	JPL 119K	AN47	JPL 147K	AN74	JPL 174K	AN103	MPJ 203L
AN20	JPL 120K	AN48	JPL 148K	AN75	JPL 175K	AN104	MPJ 204L
AN21	JPL 121K	AN49	JPL 149K	AN76	JPL 176K	AN105	MPJ 205L
AN22	JPL 122K	AN50	JPL 150K	AN77	JPL 177K	AN106	MPJ 206L
AN23	JPL 123K	AN51	JPL 151K	AN78	JPL 178K	AN107	MPJ 207L
AN24	JPL 124K	AN52	JPL 152K	AN79	JPL 179K	AN108	MPJ 208L
AN25	JPL 125K	AN53	JPL 153K	AN80	JPL 180K	AN109	MPJ 209L
AN26	JPL 126K	AN54	JPL 154K	AN81	JPL 181K	AN110	MPJ 210L
AN27	JPL 127K	AN55	JPL 155K	AN82	JPL 182K	AN111	MPJ 211L
AN28	JPL 128K	AN56	JPL 156K	AN83	JPL 183K	AN112	MPJ 212L
AN29	JPL 129K	AN57	JPL 157K	AN84	JPL 184K	AN113	MPJ 213L
AN30	JPL 130K	AN58	JPL 158K	AN85	JPL 185K	AN114	MPJ 214L
AN31	JPL 131K	AN59	JPL 159K	AN86	JPL 186K	AN115	MPJ 215L
AN32	JPL 132K	AN60	JPL 160K	AN87	JPL 187K	AN116	MPJ 216L
AN33	JPL 133K	AN61	JPL 161K	AN88	JPL 188K	AN117	MPJ 217L
AN34	JPL 134K	AN62	JPL 162K	AN89	JPL 189K	AN118	MPJ 218L
AN35	JPL 135K	AN63	JPL 163K	AN90	JPL 190K	AN119	MPJ 219L
AN36	JPL 136K	AN64	JPL 164K	AN91	MPJ 191L	AN120	MPJ 220L
AN37	JPL 137K						

AN121-123

Chassis: Leyland 'Atlantean' AN68/1R, built 1974
Body: Park Royal H43/28D

AN121	VPB 121M	AN122	VPB 122M	AN123	VPB 123M

AN124-232

Chassis: Leyland 'Atlantean' AN68A/1R, built 1978-1980
Body: (AN124-183) Park Royal H43/30F
(AN184-232) Roe H43/30F

AN124	UPK 124S	AN136	UPK 136S	AN148	VPA 148S	AN160	XPG 160T
AN125	UPK 125S	AN137	UPK 137S	AN149	VPA 149S	AN161	XPG 161T
AN126	UPK 126S	AN138	UPK 138S	AN150	VPA 150S	AN162	XPG 162T
AN127	UPK 127S	AN139	UPK 139S	AN151	VPA 151S	AN163	XPG 163T
AN128	UPK 128S	AN140	UPK 140S	AN152	VPA 152S	AN164	XPG 164T
AN129	UPK 129S	AN141	UPK 141S	AN153	VPA 153S	AN165	XPG 165T
AN130	UPK 130S	AN142	UPK 142S	AN154	VPA 154S	AN166	XPG 166T
AN131	UPK 131S	AN143	UPK 143S	AN155	VPA 155S	AN167	XPG 167T
AN132	UPK 132S	AN144	UPK 144S	AN156	VPA 156S	AN168	XPG 168T
AN133	UPK 133S	AN145	UPK 145S	AN157	VPA 157S	AN169	XPG 169T
AN134	UPK 134S	AN146	UPK 146S	AN158	VPA 158S	AN170	XPG 170T
AN135	UPK 135S	AN147	UPK 147S	AN159	XPG 159T	AN171	XPG 171T

AN172	XPG 172T	AN188	XPG 188T	AN203	EPH 203V	AN218	EPH 218V
AN173	XPG 173T	AN189	XPG 189T	AN204	EPH 204V	AN219	EPH 219V
AN174	XPG 174T	AN190	XPG 190T	AN205	EPH 205V	AN220	EPH 220V
AN175	XPG 175T	AN191	XPG 191T	AN206	EPH 206V	AN221	EPH 221V
AN176	XPG 176T	AN192	XPG 192T	AN207	EPH 207V	AN222	EPH 222V
AN177	XPG 177T	AN193	XPG 193T	AN208	EPH 208V	AN223	EPH 223V
AN178	XPG 178T	AN194	XPG 194T	AN209	EPH 209V	AN224	EPH 224V
AN179	XPG 179T	AN195	XPG 195T	AN210	EPH 210V	AN225	EPH 225V
AN180	XPG 180T	AN196	XPG 196T	AN211	EPH 211V	AN226	EPH 226V
AN181	XPG 181T	AN197	XPG 197T	AN212	EPH 212V	AN227	EPH 227V
AN182	XPG 182T	AN198	XPG 198T	AN213	EPH 213V	AN228	EPH 228V
AN183	XPG 183T	AN199	XPG 199T	AN214	EPH 214V	AN229	EPH 229V
AN184	XPG 184T	AN200	XPG 200T	AN215	EPH 215V	AN230	EPH 230V
AN185	XPG 185T	AN201	XPG 201T	AN216	EPH 216V	AN231	EPH 231V
AN186	XPG 186T	AN202	XPG 202T	AN217	EPH 217V	AN232	EPH 232V
AN187	XPG 187T						

AN233-292

Chassis: Leyland 'Atlantean' AN68B/1R, built 1980/1981
Body: Roe H43/30F

AN233	JPE 233V	AN248	KPJ 248W	AN263	KPJ 263W	AN278	KPJ 278W
AN234	JPE 234V	AN249	KPJ 249W	AN264	KPJ 264W	AN279	KPJ 279W
AN235	JPE 235V	AN250	KPJ 250W	AN265	KPJ 265W	AN280	KPJ 280W
AN236	JPE 236V	AN251	KPJ 251W	AN266	KPJ 266W	AN281	KPJ 281W
AN237	JPE 237V	AN252	KPJ 252W	AN267	KPJ 267W	AN282	KPJ 282W
AN238	KPJ 238W	AN253	KPJ 253W	AN268	KPJ 268W	AN283	KPJ 283W
AN239	KPJ 239W	AN254	KPJ 254W	AN269	KPJ 269W	AN284	KPJ 284W
AN240	KPJ 240W	AN255	KPJ 255W	AN270	KPJ 270W	AN285	KPJ 285W
AN241	KPJ 241W	AN256	KPJ 256W	AN271	KPJ 271W	AN286	KPJ 286W
AN242	KPJ 242W	AN257	KPJ 257W	AN272	KPJ 272W	AN287	KPJ 287W
AN243	KPJ 243W	AN258	KPJ 258W	AN273	KPJ 273W	AN288	KPJ 288W
AN244	KPJ 244W	AN259	KPJ 259W	AN274	KPJ 274W	AN289	KPJ 289W
AN245	KPJ 245W	AN260	KPJ 260W	AN275	KPJ 275W	AN290	KPJ 290W
AN246	KPJ 246W	AN261	KPJ 261W	AN276	KPJ 276W	AN291	KPJ 291W
AN247	KPJ 247W	AN262	KPJ 262W	AN277	KPJ 277W	AN292	KPJ 292W

AN293

Chassis: Leyland 'Atlantean' AN68C/1R, built 1981
Body: Roe H43/30F

AN293 MPG 293W

BN57-67

Chassis: Bristol LHS6L built 1977
Body: ECW B35F

BN57	TPJ 57S	BN59	TPJ 59S	BN66	TPJ 66S	BN67	TPJ 67S
BN58	TPJ 58S					

BTL1-33

Chassis: Leyland 'Tiger' TRCTL11/3RH built 1984-1985
Body: (BTL1/26-33) Berkhof C37FT
   (BTL12/14/16/18) Berkhof C49FT
   (Remainder) Berkhof C53F

BTL1	B101 KPF	BTL10	B110 KPF	BTL18	B118 KPF	BTL26	C126 PPE
BTL2	B102 KPF	BTL11	B111 KPF	BTL19	B119 KPF	BTL27	C127 PPE
BTL3	B103 KPF	BTL12	B112 KPF	BTL20	B120 KPF	BTL28	C128 PPE
BTL4	B104 KPF	BTL13	B113 KPF	BTL21	B121 KPF	BTL29	C129 PPE
BTL5	B105 KPF	BTL14	B114 KPF	BTL22	B122 KPF	BTL30	C130 PPE
BTL6	B106 KPF	BTL15	B115 KPF	BTL23	B123 KPF	BTL31	C131 PPE
BTL7	B107 KPF	BTL16	B116 KPF	BTL24	B124 KPF	BTL32	C132 PPE
BTL8	B108 KPF	BTL17	B117 KPF	BTL25	B125 KPF	BTL33	C133 PPE
BTL9	B109 KPF						

DL1-17

Chassis: Leyland 'Leopard' PSU3E/4R built 1980/1981
Body: (DL1-4/9-17) Duple C49F
(DL5-8) Duple C53F
DL6 was rebodied in 1983

DL1	HPC 101V	DL6	MPL 126W	DL10	MPL 130W	DL14	MPL 134W
DL2	HPC 102V	DL7	MPL 127W	DL11	MPL 131W	DL15	MPL 135W
DL3	MPL 123W	DL8	MPL 128W	DL12	MPL 132W	DL16	MPL 136W
DL4	MPL 124W	DL9	MPL 129W	DL13	MPL 133W	DL17	MPL 137W
DL5	MPL 125W						

DV1-2

Chassis: Volvo B58-56 built 1980
Body: Duple C53F

DV1	GPH 1V	DV2	GPH 2V

LNB24-69

Chassis and Body: Leyland National 1151/2R integral construction vehicles with C21D bodies (providing space for 8 wheelchairs in addition), built 1973
These were rebuilt from standard Nationals with B49F bodies in 1984/1985

LNB24	NPD 124L	LNB69	NPD 169L

LR1-75

Chassis: Leyland 'Olympian' ONTL11/1R built 1982-1985
Body: (LR1-60) Roe H43/29F
(LR61-75) ECW H43/29F

LR1	TPD 101X	LR20	TPD 120X	LR39	A139 DPE	LR58	A158 FPG
LR2	TPD 102X	LR21	TPD 121X	LR40	A140 DPE	LR59	A159 FPG
LR3	TPD 103X	LR22	TPD 122X	LR41	A141 DPE	LR60	A160 FPG
LR4	TPD 104X	LR23	TPD 123X	LR42	A142 DPE	LR61	B261 LPH
LR5	TPD 105X	LR24	TPD 124X	LR43	A143 DPE	LR62	B262 LPH
LR6	TPD 106X	LR25	TPD 125X	LR44	A144 DPE	LR63	B263 LPH
LR7	TPD 107X	LR26	TPD 126X	LR45	A145 DPE	LR64	B264 LPH
LR8	TPD 108X	LR27	TPD 127X	LR46	A146 FPG	LR65	B265 LPH
LR9	TPD 109X	LR28	TPD 128X	LR47	A147 FPG	LR66	B266 LPH
LR10	TPD 110X	LR29	TPD 129X	LR48	A148 FPG	LR67	B267 LPH
LR11	TPD 111X	LR30	TPD 130X	LR49	A149 FPG	LR68	B268 LPH
LR12	TPD 112X	LR31	BPF 131Y	LR50	A150 FPG	LR69	B269 LPH
LR13	TPD 113X	LR32	BPF 132Y	LR51	A151 FPG	LR70	B270 LPH
LR14	TPD 114X	LR33	BPF 133Y	LR52	A152 FPG	LR71	B271 LPH
LR15	TPD 115X	LR34	BPF 134Y	LR53	A153 FPG	LR72	B272 LPH
LR16	TPD 116X	LR35	BPF 135Y	LR54	A154 FPG	LR73	B273 LPH
LR17	TPD 117X	LR36	BPF 136Y	LR55	A155 FPG	LR74	B274 LPH
LR18	TPD 118X	LR37	BPF 137Y	LR56	A156 FPG	LR75	B275 LPH
LR19	TPD 119X	LR38	A138 DPE	LR57	A157 FPG		

LRC1-10

Chassis: Leyland 'Olympian' ONTL11/2R built 1984/1985
Body: (LRC1-5) ECW CH45/27F
(LRC6-10) ECW CH45/24F

LRC1	A101 FPL	LRC4	A104 FPL	LRC7	B107 LPH	LRC9	B109 LPH
LRC2	A102 FPL	LRC5	A105 FPL	LRC8	B108 LPH	LRC10	B110 LPH
LRC3	A103 FPL	LRC6	B106 LPH				

NTL1-2

Chassis: Leyland 'Tiger' TRCTL11/3R built 1982
Body: Plaxton C50F
Ex National Travel (London) Ltd in 1985

NTL1	SMY 629X	NTL2	SMY 630X

P1-5

Chassis: AEC 'Reliance' 6U3ZR built 1973
Body: Plaxton C49F

P1	SPK 201M	P3	SPK 203M	P4	SPK 204M	P5	SPK 205M
P2	SPK 202M						

PL18-32

Chassis: Leyland 'Leopard' PSU3E/4R built 1981
Body: Plaxton C49F (PL23/31 are C53F)

PL18	NPA 218W	PL22	NPA 222W	PL26	NPA 226W	PL30	NPA 230W
PL19	NPA 219W	PL23	NPA 223W	PL27	NPA 227W	PL31	NPA 231W
PL20	NPA 220W	PL24	NPA 224W	PL28	NPA 228W	PL32	NPA 232W
PL21	NPA 221W	PL25	NPA 225W	PL29	NPA 229W		

RN1-10

Chassis: AEC 'Reliance' 6U2R built 1972
Body: Plaxton DP60F
Ex Barton Transport PLC Nos. 1229/1220-1228 in 1977

RN1	MRR 811K	RN4	MRR 804K	RN7	MRR 807K	RN9	MRR 809K
RN2	MRR 802K	RN5	MRR 805K	RN8	MRR 808K	RN10	MRR 810K
RN3	MRR 803K	RN6	MRR 806K				

SNB71-115

Chassis and Body: Leyland National 1051/1R integral-construction vehicles with B41F bodies, built 1973/1974

SNB71	TPD 171M	SNB82	TPD 182M	SNB94	TPD 194M	SNB106	UPE 206M
SNB72	TPD 172M	SNB83	TPD 183M	SNB95	TPD 195M	SNB107	UPE 207M
SNB73	TPD 173M	SNB84	TPD 184M	SNB96	UPE 196M	SNB108	UPE 208M
SNB74	TPD 174M	SNB85	TPD 185M	SNB98	UPE 198M	SNB109	UPE 209M
SNB75	TPD 175M	SNB87	TPD 187M	SNB99	UPE 199M	SNB110	UPE 210M
SNB76	TPD 176M	SNB88	TPD 188M	SNB100	UPE 200M	SNB111	UPE 211M
SNB77	TPD 177M	SNB89	TPD 189M	SNB101	UPE 201M	SNB112	UPE 212M
SNB78	TPD 178M	SNB90	TPD 190M	SNB102	UPE 202M	SNB113	UPE 213M
SNB79	TPD 179M	SNB91	TPD 191M	SNB103	UPE 203M	SNB114	UPE 214M
SNB80	TPD 180M	SNB92	TPD 192M	SNB104	UPE 204M	SNB115	UPE 215M
SNB81	TPD 181M	SNB93	TPD 193M	SNB105	UPE 205M		

SNB116-202

Chassis and Body: Leyland National 10351/1R/SC integral-construction vehicles with DP39F bodies, built 1974-1976

SNB116	WPG 216M	SNB137	XPG 237N	SNB156	HPF 306N	SNB176	HPF 326N
SNB117	WPG 217M	SNB138	XPG 238N	SNB157	HPF 307N	SNB177	HPF 327N
SNB118	WPG 218M	SNB139	XPG 239N	SNB158	HPF 308N	SNB178	LPB 178P
SNB119	WPG 219M	SNB140	XPG 240N	SNB159	HPF 309N	SNB179	LPB 179P
SNB120	WPG 220M	SNB141	GPD 295N	SNB160	HPF 310N	SNB180	LPB 180P
SNB121	WPG 221M	SNB142	XPG 242N	SNB161	HPF 311N	SNB181	LPB 181P
SNB122	WPG 222M	SNB143	XPG 243N	SNB162	HPF 312N	SNB182	LPB 182P
SNB123	WPG 223M	SNB144	XPG 244N	SNB163	HPF 313N	SNB183	LPB 183P
SNB124	WPG 224M	SNB145	GPD 296N	SNB164	HPF 314N	SNB184	LPB 184P
SNB125	WPG 225M	SNB146	GPD 297N	SNB165	HPF 315N	SNB185	LPB 185P
SNB127	XPD 227N	SNB147	GPD 298N	SNB166	HPF 316N	SNB186	LPB 186P
SNB128	GPD 294N	SNB148	HPF 298N	SNB168	HPF 318N	SNB187	LPB 187P
SNB129	XPD 229N	SNB149	HPF 299N	SNB169	HPF 319N	SNB188	LPB 188P
SNB130	XPD 230N	SNB150	HPF 300N	SNB170	HPF 320N	SNB189	LPB 189P
SNB131	XPD 231N	SNB151	HPF 301N	SNB171	HPF 321N	SNB190	LPB 190P
SNB132	XPD 232N	SNB152	HPF 302N	SNB172	HPF 322N	SNB191	LPB 191P
SNB133	XPD 233N	SNB153	HPF 303N	SNB173	HPF 323N	SNB192	LPB 192P
SNB134	XPD 234N	SNB154	HPF 304N	SNB174	HPF 324N	SNB193	LPB 193P
SNB135	XPD 235N	SNB155	HPF 305N	SNB175	HPF 325N	SNB194	LPB 194P

SNC195	LPB 195P	SNC197	LPB 197P	SNB199	LPB 199P	SNB201	LPB 201P
SNC196	LPB 196P	SNC198	LPB 198P	SNB200	LPB 200P	SNB202	LPB 202P

SNB203-227

Chassis and Body: Leyland National 10351/1R integral construction vehicles with B41F bodies, built 1976

SNB203	LPB 203P	SNB209	LPB 209P	SNB215	LPB 215P	SNB222	LPB 222P
SNB204	LPB 204P	SNB210	LPB 210P	SNB216	LPB 216P	SNB223	LPB 223P
SNB205	LPB 205P	SNB211	LPB 211P	SNB217	LPB 217P	SNB224	LPB 224P
SNB206	LPB 206P	SNB212	LPB 212P	SNB218	LPB 218P	SNB225	LPB 225P
SNB207	LPB 207P	SNB213	LPB 213P	SNB219	LPB 219P	SNB226	LPB 226P
SNB208	LPB 208P	SNB214	LPB 214P	SNB221	LPB 221P	SNB227	LPB 227P

SNB228-375

Chassis and Body: Leyland National 10351A/1R integral-construction vehicles with B41F bodies, built 1976-1978

SNB228	NPK 228R	SNB265	SPC 265R	SNB302	UPB 302S	SNB339	UPB 339S
SNB229	NPK 229R	SNB266	SPC 266R	SNB303	UPB 303S	SNB340	UPB 340S
SNB230	NPK 230R	SNB267	SPC 267R	SNB304	UPB 304S	SNB341	UPB 341S
SNB231	NPK 231R	SNB268	SPC 268R	SNB305	UPB 305S	SNB342	UPB 342S
SNB232	NPK 232R	SNB269	SPC 269R	SNB306	UPB 306S	SNB343	UPB 343S
SNB233	NPK 233R	SNB270	SPC 270R	SNB307	UPB 307S	SNB344	UPB 344S
SNB234	NPK 234R	SNB271	SPC 271R	SNB308	UPB 308S	SNB345	UPB 345S
SNB235	NPK 235R	SNB272	SPC 272R	SNB309	UPB 309S	SNB346	UPB 346S
SNB236	NPK 236R	SNB273	SPC 273R	SNB310	UPB 310S	SNB347	UPB 347S
SNB237	NPK 237R	SNB274	SPC 274R	SNB311	UPB 311S	SNB348	UPB 348S
SNB238	NPK 238R	SNB275	SPC 275R	SNB312	UPB 312S	SNB349	UPB 349S
SNB239	NPK 239R	SNB276	SPC 276R	SNB313	UPB 313S	SNB350	UPB 350S
SNB240	NPK 240R	SNB277	SPC 277R	SNB314	UPB 314S	SNB351	UPB 351S
SNB241	NPK 241R	SNB278	SPC 278R	SNB315	UPB 315S	SNB352	UPB 352S
SNB242	NPK 242R	SNB279	SPC 279R	SNB316	UPB 316S	SNB353	UPB 353S
SNB243	NPK 243R	SNB280	SPC 280R	SNB317	UPB 317S	SNB354	XPC 14S
SNB244	NPK 244R	SNB281	SPC 281R	SNB318	UPB 318S	SNB355	XPC 15S
SNB245	NPK 245R	SNB282	SPC 282R	SNB319	UPB 319S	SNB356	XPC 16S
SNB246	NPK 246R	SNB283	SPC 283R	SNB320	UPB 320S	SNB357	XPC 17S
SNB247	NPK 247R	SNB284	SPC 284R	SNB321	UPB 321S	SNB358	YPF 758T
SNB248	NPK 248R	SNB285	SPC 285R	SNB322	UPB 322S	SNB359	YPF 759T
SNB249	NPK 249R	SNB286	SPC 286R	SNB323	UPB 323S	SNB360	YPF 760T
SNB250	NPK 250R	SNB287	SPC 287R	SNB324	UPB 324S	SNB361	YPF 761T
SNB251	NPK 251R	SNB288	SPC 288R	SNB325	UPB 325S	SNB362	YPF 762T
SNB252	NPK 252R	SNB289	SPC 289R	SNB326	UPB 326S	SNB363	YPF 763T
SNB253	NPK 253R	SNB290	SPC 290R	SNB327	UPB 327S	SNB364	YPF 764T
SNB254	NPK 254R	SNB291	SPC 291R	SNB328	UPB 328S	SNB365	YPF 765T
SNB255	NPK 255R	SNB292	TPL 292S	SNB329	UPB 329S	SNB366	YPF 766T
SNB256	NPK 256R	SNB293	TPL 293S	SNB330	UPB 330S	SNB367	YPF 767T
SNB257	NPK 257R	SNB294	UPB 294S	SNB331	UPB 331S	SNB368	YPF 768T
SNB258	NPK 258R	SNB295	UPB 295S	SNB332	UPB 332S	SNB369	YPF 769T
SNB259	NPK 259R	SNB296	UPB 296S	SNB333	UPB 333S	SNB370	YPF 770T
SNB260	NPK 260R	SNB297	UPB 297S	SNB334	UPB 334S	SNB371	YPF 771T
SNB261	NPK 261R	SNB298	UPB 298S	SNB335	UPB 335S	SNB372	YPF 772T
SNB262	NPK 262R	SNB299	UPB 299S	SNB336	UPB 336S	SNB373	YPF 773T
SNB263	NPK 263R	SNB300	UPB 300S	SNB337	UPB 337S	SNB374	YPF 774T
SNB264	SPC 264R	SNB301	UPB 301S	SNB338	UPB 338S	SNB375	YPF 775T

SNB376-543

Chassis and Body: Leyland National 10351B/1R integral-construction vehicles with B41F bodies, built 1978/1979

SNB376	YPL 376T	SNB378	YPL 378T	SNB380	YPL 380T	SNB382	YPL 382T
SNB377	YPL 377T	SNB379	YPL 379T	SNB381	YPL 381T	SNB383	YPL 383T

SNB384	YPL 384T	SNB424	YPL 424T	SNB464	BPL 464T	SNB504	EPD 504V
SNB385	YPL 385T	SNB425	YPL 425T	SNB465	BPL 465T	SNB505	EPD 505V
SNB386	YPL 386T	SNB426	YPL 426T	SNB466	BPL 466T	SNB506	EPD 506V
SNB387	YPL 387T	SNB427	YPL 427T	SNB467	BPL 467T	SNB507	EPD 507V
SNB388	YPL 388T	SNB428	YPL 428T	SNB468	BPL 468T	SNB508	EPD 508V
SNB389	YPL 389T	SNB429	YPL 429T	SNB469	BPL 469T	SNB509	EPD 509V
SNB390	YPL 390T	SNB430	YPL 430T	SNB470	BPL 470T	SNB510	EPD 510V
SNB391	YPL 391T	SNB431	YPL 431T	SNB471	BPL 471T	SNB511	EPD 511V
SNB392	YPL 392T	SNB432	YPL 432T	SNB472	BPL 472T	SNB512	EPD 512V
SNB393	YPL 393T	SNB433	YPL 433T	SNB473	BPL 473T	SNB513	EPD 513V
SNB394	YPL 394T	SNB434	YPL 434T	SNB474	BPL 474T	SNB514	EPD 514V
SNB395	YPL 395T	SNB435	YPL 435T	SNB475	BPL 475T	SNB515	EPD 515V
SNB396	YPL 396T	SNB436	YPL 436T	SNB476	BPL 476T	SNB516	EPD 516V
SNB397	YPL 397T	SNB437	YPL 437T	SNB477	BPL 477T	SNB517	EPD 517V
SNB398	YPL 398T	SNB438	YPL 438T	SNB478	BPL 478T	SNB518	EPD 518V
SNB399	YPL 399T	SNB439	YPL 439T	SNB479	BPL 479T	SNB519	EPD 519V
SNB400	YPL 400T	SNB440	YPL 440T	SNB480	BPL 480T	SNB520	EPD 520V
SNB401	YPL 401T	SNB441	YPL 441T	SNB481	BPL 481T	SNB521	EPD 521V
SNB402	YPL 402T	SNB442	YPL 442T	SNB482	BPL 482T	SNB522	EPD 522V
SNB403	YPL 403T	SNB443	YPL 443T	SNB483	BPL 483T	SNB523	EPD 523V
SNB404	YPL 404T	SNB444	YPL 444T	SNB484	BPL 484T	SNB524	EPD 524V
SNB405	YPL 405T	SNB445	YPL 445T	SNB485	BPL 485T	SNB525	EPD 525V
SNB406	YPL 406T	SNB446	YPL 446T	SNB486	BPL 486T	SNB526	EPD 526V
SNB407	YPL 407T	SNB447	YPL 447T	SNB487	BPL 487T	SNB527	EPD 527V
SNB408	YPL 408T	SNB448	YPL 448T	SNB488	BPL 488T	SNB528	EPD 528V
SNB409	YPL 409T	SNB449	YPL 449T	SNB489	BPL 489T	SNB529	EPD 529V
SNB410	YPL 410T	SNB450	YPL 450T	SNB490	BPL 490T	SNB530	EPD 530V
SNB411	YPL 411T	SNB451	YPL 451T	SNB491	BPL 491T	SNB531	EPD 531V
SNE412	YPL 412T	SNB452	YPL 452T	SNB492	BPL 492T	SNB532	EPD 532V
SNB413	YPL 413T	SNB453	YPL 453T	SNB493	BPL 493T	SNB533	EPD 533V
SNB414	YPL 414T	SNB454	YPL 454T	SNB494	BPL 494T	SNB534	EPD 534V
SNB415	YPL 415T	SNB455	YPL 455T	SNB495	BPL 495T	SNB535	EPD 535V
SNB416	YPL 416T	SNB456	YPL 456T	SNB496	BPL 496T	SNB536	EPD 536V
SNB417	YPL 417T	SNB457	YPL 457T	SNB497	BPL 497T	SNB537	EPD 537V
SNB418	YPL 418T	SNB458	YPL 458T	SNB498	BPL 498T	SNB538	EPD 538V
SNB419	YPL 419T	SNB459	BPL 459T	SNB499	DPH 499T	SNB539	EPD 539V
SNE420	YPL 420T	SNB460	BPL 460T	SNB500	DPH 500T	SNB540	EPD 540V
SNB421	YPL 421T	SNB461	BPL 461T	SNB501	DPH 501T	SNB541	EPD 541V
SNB422	YPL 422T	SNB462	BPL 462T	SNB502	DPH 502T	SNB542	EPD 542V
SNB423	YPL 423T	SNB463	BPL 463T	SNB503	DPH 503T	SNB543	EPD 543V

STL1-12

Chassis: Leyland 'Tiger' TRCTL11/3RH built 1985
Body: Plaxton C51F (convertible to C49FT)

STL1	C201 PPE	STL4	C204 PPE	STL7	C207 PPE	STL10	C210 PPE
STL2	C202 PPE	STL5	C205 PPE	STL8	C208 PPE	STL11	C211 PPE
STL3	C203 PPE	STL6	C206 PPE	STL9	C209 PPE	STL12	C212 PPE

TD1-45

Chassis: Leyland 'Tiger' TRCTL11/2R built 1983
Body: (TD1-8/10-14/17-20/22/39-45) Duple C53F
         (TD9/15/16/21/23-28) Duple C49F
         (TD29-38) Duple C46F

TD1	YPD 101Y	TD9	YPD 109Y	TD17	YPD 117Y	TD25	YPD 125Y
TD2	YPD 102Y	TD10	YPD 110Y	TD18	YPD 118Y	TD26	YPD 126Y
TD3	YPD 103Y	TD11	YPD 111Y	TD19	YPD 119Y	TD27	YPD 127Y
TD4	YPD 104Y	TD12	YPD 112Y	TD20	YPD 120Y	TD28	YPD 128Y
TD5	YPD 105Y	TD13	YPD 113Y	TD21	YPD 121Y	TD29	YPD 129Y
TD6	YPD 106Y	TD14	YPD 114Y	TD22	YPD 122Y	TD30	YPD 130Y
TD7	YPD 107Y	TD15	YPD 115Y	TD23	YPD 123Y	TD31	YPD 131Y
TD8	YPD 108Y	TD16	YPD 116Y	TD24	YPD 124Y	TD32	YPD 132Y

TD33	YPD 133Y	TD37	YPD 137Y	TD40	YPD 140Y	TD43	YPD 143Y
TD34	YPD 134Y	TD38	YPD 138Y	TD41	YPD 141Y	TD44	YPD 144Y
TD35	YPD 135Y	TD39	YPD 139Y	TD42	YPD 142Y	TD45	YPD 145Y
TD36	YPD 136Y						

TL1-42

Chassis: Leyland 'Tiger' TRCTL11/2R built 1982
Body: (TL1-30) ECW C49F
(TL31-42) ECW C53F

TL1	TPC 101X	TL12	WPH 112Y	TL23	WPH 123Y	TL33	WPH 133Y
TL2	TPC 102X	TL13	TPC 113X	TL24	WPH 124Y	TL34	WPH 134Y
TL3	TPC 103X	TL14	TPC 114X	TL25	WPH 125Y	TL35	WPH 135Y
TL4	TPC 104X	TL15	WPH 115Y	TL26	WPH 126Y	TL36	WPH 136Y
TL5	TPC 105X	TL16	WPH 116Y	TL27	WPH 127Y	TL37	WPH 137Y
TL6	TPC 106X	TL17	WPH 117Y	TL28	WPH 128Y	TL38	WPH 138Y
TL7	TPC 107X	TL18	WPH 118Y	TL29	WPH 129Y	TL39	WPH 139Y
TL8	TPC 108X	TL19	WPH 119Y	TL30	WPH 130Y	TL40	WPH 140Y
TL9	TPC 109X	TL20	WPH 120Y	TL31	WPH 131Y	TL41	WPH 141Y
TL10	TPC 110X	TL21	WPH 121Y	TL32	WPH 132Y	TL42	WPH 142Y
TL11	TPC 111X	TL22	WPH 122Y				

TP1-40

Chassis: Leyland 'Tiger' TRCTL11/2R built 1983/1984
Body: (TP1-29/36-40) Plaxton C53F
(TP30) Plaxton C48FT
(TP31-35) Plaxton C49F

TP1	A101 EPA	TP11	A111 EPA	TP21	A121 EPA	TP31	A131 EPA
TP2	A102 EPA	TP12	A112 EPA	TP22	A122 EPA	TP32	A132 EPA
TP3	A103 EPA	TP13	A113 EPA	TP23	A123 EPA	TP33	A133 EPA
TP4	A104 EPA	TP14	A114 EPA	TP24	A124 EPA	TP34	A134 EPA
TP5	A105 EPA	TP15	A115 EPA	TP25	A125 EPA	TP35	A135 EPA
TP6	A106 EPA	TP16	A116 EPA	TP26	A126 EPA	TP36	A136 EPA
TP7	A107 EPA	TP17	A117 EPA	TP27	A127 EPA	TP37	A137 EFA
TP8	A108 EPA	TP18	A118 EPA	TP28	A128 EPA	TP38	A138 EPA
TP9	A109 EPA	TP19	A119 EPA	TP29	A129 EPA	TP39	A139 EPA
TP10	A110 EPA	TP20	A120 EPA	TP30	A130 EPA	TP40	A140 EPA

TPL41-60

Chassis: Leyland 'Tiger' TRCTL11/3R built 1984
Body: Plaxton C51F (TPL58-60 are C50FT)

TPL41	A141 EPA	TPL46	A146 EPA	TPL51	A151 EPA	TPL56	A156 EPA
TPL42	A142 EPA	TPL47	A147 EPA	TPL52	A152 EPA	TPL57	A157 EPA
TPL43	A143 EPA	TPL48	A148 EPA	TPL53	A153 EPA	TPL58	A158 EPA
TPL44	A144 EPA	TPL49	A149 EPA	TPL54	A154 EPA	TPL59	A159 EPA
TPL45	A145 EPA	TPL50	A150 EPA	TPL55	A155 EPA	TPL6C	A160 EPA

TP61-75

Chassis: Leyland 'Tiger' TRCTL11/2R built 1985
Body: Plaxton C49F

TP61	B261 KPF	TP65	B265 KFF	TP69	B269 KPF	TP73	B273 KPF
TP62	B262 KPF	TF66	B266 KPF	TP70	B270 KPF	TP74	B274 KPF
TP63	B263 KPF	TP67	B267 KPF	TP71	B271 KPF	TP75	B275 KPF
TP64	B264 KPF	TP68	B268 KPF	TP72	B272 KPF		

TPL76-84

Chassis: Leyland 'Tiger' TRCTL11/3RH built 1985
Body: Plaxton C53F

TPL76	B276 KPF	TPL79	B279 KPF	TPL81	B281 KPF	TPL83	B283 KPF
TPL77	B277 KPF	TPL80	B280 KPF	TPL82	B282 KPF	TPL84	B284 KPF
TPL78	B278 KPF						

TPL85-95 Chassis: Leyland 'Tiger' TRCTL11/3R built 1985
Body: (TPL85-90) Plaxton C50FT
        (TPL91-95) Plaxton C51F

TPL85	B285 KPF	TPL88	B288 KPF	TPL91	B291 KPF	TPL94	B294 KPF
TPL86	B286 KPF	TPL89	B289 KPF	TPL92	B292 KPF	TPL95	B295 KPF
TPL87	B287 KPF	TPL90	B290 KPF	TPL93	B293 KPF		

Metrobus Ltd

The East Croydon to Orpington bus services have been operated by a series of independent firms, with no London Transport involvement at any time. They were started in 1969 by North Downs Rural Transport, later passing to Orpington & District Omnibuses under the ownership of Miss J M Normington. She built up a fleet of 10 vehicles, 7 of them double-deckers. However, financial pressures were experienced by Orpington & District as they had been by North Downs, and the largely rural route from Croydon to Orpington (and the even more rural minibus route from Orpington to Biggin Hill) were not sufficiently profitable to keep the enterprise afloat.

In early 1981 Orpington & District ceased trading and its vehicles were sold. On 2nd March 1981 the service was taken over by the Tillingbourne Bus Co of Cranleigh, Surrey, which formed a new subsidiary, Tillingbourne (Metropolitan) Ltd, to run the Croydon - Orpington route. Single-deckers, mainly coaches, were allocated to this company, but one double-decker - the only one ever owned by Tillingbourne - was also acquired.

In September 1983 a new company, Metrobus Ltd, was created by two directors of Tillingbourne (Metropolitan) Ltd. It took over the Croydon - Forestdale and Croydon - Orpington routes, together with six vehicles including the double-decker. The routes, numbered 853/855/857 under Orpington & District, were renumbered 353/355/357 on takeover by Tillingbourne, and these numbers are retained by Metrobus. 353 runs direct from East Croydon Station to Orpington; 355 goes from East Croydon to Forestdale Estate; and 357 is a weekend diversion of the 353 which visits Forestdale Estate en route from Croydon to Orpington. An occasional service 354 runs from Croydon via Forestdale and Hayes to Bromley. The whole network is within Greater London, although the Forestdale terminus is right on the boundary. Except for the Orpington - Farnborough section and short lengths in Hayes and Addington, hardly any of the roads used have ever been served by LT. Metrobus has moved the old Altyre Road, Croydon, terminus, a quiet back street near East Croydon Station, to a more central location at the Fairfield Halls. A summer excursion service links Orpington, New Addington, Sanderstead, Purley and Coulsdon to Brighton and Worthing.

The headquarters and garage of Metrobus Ltd is at Oak Farm, Farnborough Hill, Green Street Green.

Regn. Number	Chassis Make and Type	Body Make and Seats	Date New	Notes
BHL 609K	Daimler 'Fleetline' CRG6LX	N Counties H43/33F	1972	(a)
BHL 624K	"	"	"	(a)
WKE 67S	Bedford YMT	Duple B61F	1978	(b)
BNO 701T	"	Duple C53F	1979	(c)

Regn. Number	Chassis Make and Type	Body Make and Seats	Date New	Notes
XPL 889T	Bedford YMT	Duple B61F	1978	(d)
ODV 404W	AEC 'Reliance' 6U2R	Duple C53F	1981	(e)
ODV 405W	"	"	"	(e)
C395 DML	Leyland 'Olympian' ONLXB/1R	ECW H43/34F	1985	

NOTES:-
(a) BHL 609/624K were ex West Riding Automobile Co Nos. 709/724 in 1984
(b) WKE 67S was ex Maidstone Borough Council No. 67 in 1985
(c) BNO 701T was ex Eastern National Omnibus Co No. 1215, via Goldenport, London SW16, in 1985
(d) XPL 889T was ex Tillingbourne (Sussex) Ltd, Cranleigh, in 1983
(e) ODV 404/405W were received on long-term lease from Tillingbourne (Metropolitan) Ltd, Cranleigh, in 1983

Mole Valley Transport Services

In September 1968 Mr M C Ash began the minibus business which was to grow into Mole Valley Services, from an address at 101 Woodgate Avenue, Chessington, Surrey. The first route operated was a fairly short link from Cobham to Downside. In August 1971 the Mole Valley fleetname was adopted, and the Downside route was numbered 815 at the same time, following a fashion among Outer London's independent stage operators to adopt service numbers avoiding clashes with LT or LCBS routes. Also in 1971 a Cobham - Oxshott - Epsom route (numbered 816) was tried, but this lasted only a few years. In August 1973 the business moved to its second home, at 30 Brighton Road, Surbiton; it moved yet again in September 1975 to Church Street, Esher. The latest move, to the present address at 37 Bridge Street, Leatherhead, took place in June 1980.

On 29th November 1975, Mole Valley took over London Country route 416 which ran from Leatherhead to Esher; this became Mole Valley route 1. The Cobham - Downside route became service 2. Several other routes were tried including a service to Chessington Zoo, but perhaps the most successful working was the extension of the Leatherhead - Esher route into Kingston-upon-Thames.

However, this (service 7) was affected by cuts in County Council revenue support, and from July 1985 it was curtailed to run between Hampton Court and Kingston, via Thames Ditton and Surbiton, only; three round trips are operated in the mornings on Mondays, Thursdays and Fridays only. This loss of work for Mole Valley was more than offset, however, by the takeover of the Hersham - Walton-on-Thames route (service 1) formerly operated by Ben Stanley Ltd of Hersham, who ceased trading in the spring of 1985. This route had been started in 1978 as a replacement for part of former LT route 264. It runs at approximately 45-minute intervals on Mondays to Saturdays, and keeps one bus busy throughout the day. It was taken over by Mole Valley on 24th July 1985 at short notice, at the County Council's request; three months later, on 26th October, Mole Valley extended the route at the Walton end to serve the Vicarage Fields Estate. The only other regular working is a school journey (service S6) which runs on schooldays from Stoke D'Abernon to Thames Ditton via Oxshott, Esher and Lower Green.

Regn. Number	Chassis Make and Type	Body Make and Seats	Date New	Notes
LGD 347V	Ford A	Dormobile C21F	1979	(a)
FNM 739Y	Ford A0610	Mellor B20F	1983	

NOTES:-
(a) LGD 347V was ex National Blood Transfusion Service, Glasgow (non-PSV) in 1985

A Moore and Sons (Windsor) Ltd

Among the green London Country and red Alder Valley buses seen in the royal borough of Windsor, the brown and cream Imperial buses are often found. A Moore & Sons started as a partnership in 1917, becoming a limited company in 1946. In the meantime the firm had participated with other independents in a service between Slough and Windsor, which they lost with one bus to the LPTB in 1933. In 1928 a route was started from Windsor Castle to the western outskirts of Windsor; gradually it was extended into the growing suburbs, and new branches were established. Finally the two main branches met at Ruddlesway, and the present circular services (clockwise service 'A' and anti-clockwise service 'B') were established. Buses run every 20 minutes in each direction on weekdays, reducing to every 40 minutes in the evenings and on Sunday afternoons; there is no Sunday morning service. Recently a direct service has been run between Ruddlesway and the town centre, inward during the morning peak and outward at lunchtime and during the evening peak.

Some buses carry both letters and numbers on their blinds, e.g. 'A1', 'B2', but the second digit indicates the duty number - an interesting variant of the London Country 'running number' system, and most unusual for a small firm. The buses operate on an 'exact fare' system using fareboxes, without issuing tickets.

The garage and office is situated at Firs Avenue, Clewer Hill Road, Windsor.

Regn. Number	Chassis Make and Type	Body Make and Seats	Date New	Notes
FLD 394C	Bedford SB3	Strachan B41F	1965	(a)
YHA 300J	Ford R192	Plaxton B45F	1970	(b)
YHA 314J	"	"	"	(b)
GRD 131L	Bedford YRQ	Duple C43F	1972	
HJH 339L	Bedford YRT	Duple C45F	"	(c)
NRX 466L	Bedford YRQ	Duple C41F	1973	
NRX 467L	"	"	"	
SWY 335L	Bedford YRT	Willowbrook B55F	1972	(d)
BMB 116M	"	Duple C53F	1974	(e)
PTM 649M	Ford R1014	Willowbrook B52F	"	
GNH 530N	Bedford YRQ	Willowbrook B45F	"	(f)
GNV 978N	"	"	"	(g)
GNV 983N	"	"	"	(f)
JHL 318P	"	Willowbrook B47F	1975	(h)
LVV 123P	Bedford YRT	Willowbrook B53F	1976	(f)
JMJ 633V	Bedford YMT	Plaxton C53F	1979	

NOTES:-
(a) FLD 394C was ex MacMillan Bloedal, London W7 (non-PSV) in 1977, but did not enter service with Moore's until 1979

(b) YHA 300/314J were ex Midland Red Omnibus Co Ltd Nos. 6300/6314 in 1978; YHA 314J did not enter service with Moore's until 1979
(c) HJH 339L was ex Fage, West Kingsdown, in 1979, but did not enter service with Moore's until 1980
(d) SWY 335L was ex Wigmore, Dinnington, in 1981
(e) BMB 116M was ex Taylor, Sutton Scotney, in 1980
(f) GNH 530N, GNV 983N and LVV 123P were ex Garratt, Syston in 1984
(g) GNV 978N was ex United Counties Omnibus Co No. 180 in 1983
(h) JHL 318P was ex Mowbray (Diamond Bus Service), Stanley, No. 44 in 1980

Mullany's Coaches and Car Hire

Mr J P Mullany of 35 Copsewood Road, Watford, Herts, founded Mullany's Coaches and Car Hire in November 1968, as a private-hire and contract operator. The business gradually grew from the one vehicle owned at the outset, to a fleet of about ten. In 1972 the trading address was moved to 1 Knutsford Avenue, Watford, and in 1981 there was a further move to Clarendon Garage, Cardiff Road, Watford.

In 1984 Mullany's took over the Watford - Elstree Aerodrome stage service from Campbell Consultants Ltd of Watford, with several vehicles. Campbell Consultants had been formed in May 1975 to take over two Watford-based companies – H & C Transport Ltd and Knightswood Coaches Ltd. From Knightswood came Campbell's only stage route, between Watford and Elstree Aerodrome, with one round trip on Tuesdays, Fridays and Saturdays. Knightswood had started this service in 1964, to serve a few isolated settlements which had never had a bus service before. In November 1977 Campbell Consultants started an experimental service from Elstree Aerodrome to Borehamwood, but this lasted for only three months.

In the summer of 1984 Mullany's introduced a route from Watford to Aldenham Country Park. This ran four round trips on Sundays and Bank Holidays only, starting on the Spring Bank Holiday weekend and ending with the August Bank Holiday weekend. The service worked on a similar basis in 1985, and will operate in future years subject to the County Council giving it financial support.

Regn. Number	Chassis Make and Type	Body Make and Seats	Date New	Notes
5513 H	Volvo B58-61	Plaxton C57F	1978	(a)
290 WE	Volvo B58-56	Plaxton C49F	"	(a)
WLJ 570K	Ford R226	Plaxton C49F	1972	(b)
GWO 910L	Ford R192	Duple C45F	1973	(c)
RDH 633M	Ford R1114	Duple C53F	1974	(d)
GHY 903N	AEC 'Reliance' 6U3ZR	Duple C57F	1975	(a)
PPE 673R	Ford R1114	Plaxton C53F	1977	(e)
WBM 145S	Ford 'Transit'	Tricentrol 12-seat	1978	(f)
WLJ 212S	Ford R1014	Plaxton C41F	"	(g)
DUE 653T	Ford R1114	Duple C53F	1979	(h)
FWD 26T	Ford 'Transit'	Tricentrol 12-seat	"	(i)
GGD 669T	Volvo B58-61	Plaxton C57F	"	(j)
HFX 410V	Ford R1114	Plaxton C53F	1980	(k)

NOTES:-
(a) 5513 H, 290 WE and GHY 903N were ex Campbell Consultants, Watford, in 1984; 5513 H and 290 WE were re-registered by Campbell in 1983, and were previously registered DWP 2S and UDT 312S respectively

"Ralph's Coaches" is almost a misnomer, for these 26 Plaxton "Bustler" bodied Fords form well over half the fleet strength. 2 (XNK 193X), one of twelve fitted with single-entrance bodywork and 47 seats, is seen appropriately "bustling" along Heathrow's North Perimeter Road on staff bus duties.

Red Rover of Aylesbury has six secondhand Leyland Nationals, the survivors of a somewhat larger fleet, which are frequently seen on the town's local bus services. Ex-Nottingham 146 (GAU 727L) is the oldest remaining example, and is about to negotiate the roundabout at the junction of Bicester and Buckingham Roads on its way into the town centre.

Set in one of Hertfordshire's most attractive villages, Richmond's coach garage itself has a timeless air about it! Any suspicion, however, that the company is not "up to the minute" would be dispelled by a look at the fleet. Ford/Duple PNM 673W, not yet six years old but already one of the older coaches in stock, demonstrates the point.

UGB 14R is a third-hand vehicle with Safeguard of Guildford, its present owners, having previously worked for Hutchison's of Overtown in Scotland and (briefly) for Tillingbourne of Cranleigh. It is also the first AEC 'Reliance' to bear the Safeguard colours since the firm's own 'Reliances' disappeared many years ago. It was photographed at Guildford Park shops, near the Safeguard garage.

London Transport's 'BL' class of Bristol LHs have provided rolling stock for many independent firms. Probably only one of them, Smith's of Buntingford, runs its specimen in LT red with an authentic LT fleet number transfer (BL38)! As a concession to its true owners however, KJD 438P, seen at the Buntingford garage, does carry "Smith's" fleetnames on the sides.

Yet another Bristol LH shares the duties on Tate's "B & B" services in the Potten End area with one of a number of coaches. VPN 6S, a 1977-vintage Plaxton-bodied Bedford YMT and one of the oldest vehicles still running with Tate's, approaches the bus stop at Potten End village green on the daily run to Hemel Hempstead.

38

Golden Miller of Feltham bought the first three Volvo B58 coaches, numerically speaking, to appear in the London area. Now under new management in the Telling's group, it is only right and proper that the Golden Miller front-line coach fleet should consist of six of these superb Volvo B10Ms with Van Hool bodies. B916 BGA was seen paying a visit to the Telling's garage at Byfleet.

Tillingbourne's rolling stock has come a long way - not just in mileage! - since the GSs shown overleaf were its basic vehicle type. The modern bus fleet now includes four Dennis buses bodied by Wadham Stringer, of which FOD 943Y, a Dennis "Dorchester", was photographed at the Cranleigh garage. It would never have fitted inside the Trices' old garage in Chilworth!

Like many leading coach companies, Tourmaster runs many of its coaches in contract liveries for major tour operators. 18 Bova coaches have been bought in the last few years, of which all but a few now have "cherished" registrations. One of the exceptions is B250 YKX, seen wearing Global Tours livery and on duty in its home town of Dunstable.

As noted previously, ECW bodywork has never been as common in Outer London as in some other areas served by former BTC bus companies. This page shows three of the exceptions. Ex-Thames Valley Bristol L6B DMO 668 was lengthened to 30 feet and fitted with a new ECW full-front body before being sold to Moore's of Windsor – one of the last "heavyweight" vehicles in service with Moore's.

84 Guy "Vixen" chassis were fitted with specially-designed ECW bodies for LT Country Area and entered service in the early 1950s. Many of them enjoyed an "afterlife" with independent firms, including eight which went to Tillingbourne Valley of Chilworth. MXX 384 was seen with its new owners in the old Onslow Street bus station in Guildford.

ECW's Lowestoft works has seldom turned out "one-off" vehicles, but this is one of the most celebrated exceptions! RMC4, the prototype coach "Routemaster", was bodied by ECW in a style closely resembling the Park Royal product. It is seen on service at Eccleston Bridge, Victoria, in LT days; it has since been officially preserved by LCBS.

(b) WLJ 570K was ex Ladvale, Dursley, circa 1985
(c) GWO 910L was ex Jeyes, Luton, in 1978
(d) RDH 633M was ex FHW, Willenhall, in 1981
(e) PPE 673R was ex Ward, Epping, in 1978
(f) WBM 145S was ex Lockwood, High Wycombe, in 1984
(g) WLJ 212S was ex Continental Coach, London SW5, circa 1982
(h) DUE 653T was ex Bradley, London E10, in 1983
(i) FWD 26T was ex Mellows, London N7, in 1982
(j) GGD 669T was ex Safford, Little Gransden, in 1985
(k) HFX 410V was ex Excelsior Holidays, Bournemouth, in 1982

Ralph's Coaches Ltd

Ralph's Coaches Ltd grew out of a car hire enterprise started by the founder, Mr R E Arrigoni, at West Drayton about 1965. By May 1971 Mr Arrigoni had bought a full-sized coach - a secondhand Bedford VAL14 - and was operating from Coldharbour Lane, Hayes, under the trading name of "Edwards Car and Coach Hire", in succession to the Embassy Coaches business of Mr H W Edwards of Hayes. In 1972 the VAL was replaced by a brand-new Ford R226.

In February 1974 the business was incorporated as a limited company, Ralph's Coaches Ltd, and moved to Old Bath Road, Longford. Only one coach was transferred to the new company, but by 1976 the fleet strength had risen to five - four full-sized Ford coaches in Sheraton Heathrow Hotel livery, and one Ford 'Transit' minibus. The hotel livery was one of several cases of coach operators around Heathrow running 'courtesy coaches' for hotels around the Airport. Ralph's also took over the coaching work for the Skyline and Heathrow Penta Hotels.

In 1981 the British Airports Authority re-awarded the contract for providing internal 'landside' transport at Heathrow Airport, which had been held by Whyte's Airport Services Ltd since the 1960s. Ralph's was the successful applicant, and bought a fleet of 24 Fords with Plaxton 'Bustler' bodies. These arrived in October 1981, more than doubling the fleet strength. Unlike the rest of Ralph's fleet, these buses carry fleet numbers for identification within the Airport. Half of them have the three-doorway layout, with perimeter seating for 29, similar to Whyte's buses which had been used on similar duties. They operate services linking the different terminal and other buildings within the Heathrow Airport complex.

Shortly after winning the Heathrow Airport contract, the company moved to Middle Green Industrial Estate, Middle Green Road, Slough.

Fleet No.	Regn. Number	Chassis Make and Type	Body Make and Seats	Date New	Notes
	APH 531T	Ford R1114	Duple C53F	1979	
	APH 532T	"	"	"	
	EPC 895V	"	"	1980	
	EPC 896V	"	"	"	
	NRO 265V	Ford/Tricentrol R1014	Duple C35F	"	
	NRO 266V	"	"	"	
	NAY 429W	Ford R1114	Caetano C53F	"	(a)
1	XNK 192X	Ford R1014	Plaxton B47F	1981	
2	XNK 193X	"	"	"	
3	XNK 194X	"	"	"	
4	XNK 195X	"	"	"	

Fleet No.	Regn. Number	Chassis Make and Type	Body Make and Seats	Date New	Notes
5	XNK 196X	Ford R1014	Plaxton B47F	1981	
6	XNK 197X	"	"	"	
7	XNK 198X	"	"	"	
8	XNK 199X	"	"	"	
9	XNK 200X	"	"	"	
10	XNK 201X	"	"	"	
11	XNK 202X	"	"	"	
12	XNK 203X	"	"	"	
13	XNK 204X	"	Plaxton B29D	"	(b)
14	XNK 205X	"	"	"	(b)
15	XNK 206X	"	"	"	(b)
16	XNK 207X	"	"	"	(b)
17	XNK 208X	"	"	"	(b)
18	XNK 209X	"	"	"	(b)
19	XNK 210X	"	"	"	(b)
20	XNK 211X	"	"	"	(b)
21	XNK 212X	"	"	"	(b)
22	XNK 213X	"	"	"	(b)
23	XNK 214X	"	"	"	(b)
24	XNK 215X	"	"	"	(b)
	YMJ 411X	Ford R1114	Plaxton C53F	1982	
25	BMJ 401X	Ford R1014	Plaxton B29D	"	(b)
26	BMJ 402X	"	"	"	(b)
	JNO 52Y	Ford R1015	Wadham Stringer DP42F	1983	
	RME 971Y	Volvo B10M-61	Plaxton C42FT	"	
	RME 972Y	"	"	"	
	RME 973Y	"	Wadham Stringer DP42F	"	
	RME 974Y	"	Plaxton C42FT	"	
	RMH 869Y	Volvo B57	Wadham Stringer DP42F	"	
	A365 DAW	Quest 80B	Locomotors B28D	1984	
	A941 VMH	Volvo B10M-61	Plaxton C53F	1983	
	A942 VMH	"	"	"	
	A943 VMH	"	"	"	
	A700 XMH	"	"	1984	
	A701 XMH	"	"	"	
	A702 XMH	"	"	"	
	A703 XMH	"	"	"	

NOTES:-
(a) NAY 429W was exhibited at the 1980 Motor Show
(b) 13-26 (XNK 204-215X, BMJ 401/402X) have front and centre nearside doors and a centre offside door; perimeter seating is fitted

Red Rover Omnibus Ltd

On 22nd July 1924, Mr Edward Cain introduced an open-top double-deck Dennis bus on London services 14 and 49. Only one bus was ever operated at a time, but the original bus was succeeded by two more Dennises before London operations were taken over by the LPTB in 1934. The business was registered as a limited company, Red Rover Omnibus Ltd, on 28th July 1927.

In 1928 an Aylesbury-based operation was started with an express coach service to

London, but this lasted only until 1932, when it became part of the Green Line coach network under London General Country Services Ltd. However, services were also started from Aylesbury, which became the firm's base after the London area operations were lost, to Buckingham, North Marston and Weedon.

The firm continued to standardise on Dennis buses, and the last acquisition of this make was bought as late as 1953, a Dennis 'Lance' K3 double-decker. Two Daimler austerity double-deckers had seen the Company through the Second World War. At the end of 1955 the Cain family, the firm's founders, retired from the business and sold it to Keith Garages Ltd of Aylesbury; the two associated fleets of Red Rover and Keith Garages continued side by side until they were merged, but Keith Coaches is still used as the trading name of the tours business, and the coaches carry dual 'Red Rover - Keith Garages' fleetnames.

The present daily services run from Aylesbury to Westcott (1), Buckingham (2), Brill and Oakley (3), Calvert (15) Bicester (16) and Edgcott (17). There are also services on Wednesdays and Saturdays to Brill and Oakley (3), on Wednesdays to Ambrosden (516) and on Tuesdays to Milton Keynes (517). Aylesbury itself is served by local services 9, 10, 12, 13 and 14, of which service 9 links Aylesbury to Stoke Mandeville Hospital. Recent developments have included Thursday services 18 and 20 for Wendover Market, and a daily service between Aldbury, Tring and New Mill - not to mention free buses from many of the surrounding villages, and from Aylesbury itself, to the Tesco hypermarket at Broadfields. All this is operated from a base in a town served by no less than four NBC subsidiaries, one of which has a local garage!

The Company also operates several South Coast express services and a programme of British and Continental excursions and tours. The Company claims to have been the first undertaking in Britain to put its coach seat booking arrangements on to a computer, which charts passengers' bookings and prints out tickets.

The coaches comprise AEC 'Reliances', Leyland 'Leopards' and Bedfords, all bought new. The service buses are mostly bought secondhand and include Leyland Nationals from various sources, and ex-London Transport DMS-type Daimler 'Fleetlines'. In the autumn of 1985 the directors decided to progressively close down the coaching side of the business and to concentrate on the highly successful stage carriage operations. In the next few months after we have gone to press, therefore, coaches nos. 114/130/131/136/137/143-145/149-151/158/159 in the following lists are likely to be offered for sale; this will leave only three coaches in the fleet, to enable the Company to cover its bus service duties adequately.

The head office is at 30 Buckingham Street, Aylesbury, and the garage is in Bicester Road. Fleet livery is red and yellow.

Fleet No.	Regn. Number	Chassis Make and Type	Body Make and Seats	Date New	Notes
114	NBW 11P	Leyland 'Leopard' PSU3C/4R	Plaxton C49F	1975	
126	AJO 311R	"	"	1977	
127	DAU 358C	AEC 'Renown' 3B3RA	Weymann H40/30F	1965	(a)
130	HUD 648S	Bedford YMT	Caetano C53F	1977	
131	HUD 649S	"	"	"	
136	SJO 870T	"	Plaxton C49F	1979	
137	SJO 871T	"	"	"	
140	MLK 419L	Daimler 'Fleetline' CRG6LXB	Park Royal H44/27D	1972	(b)
141	BBW 141V	Bedford YMT	Plaxton C53F	1979	
142	BBW 142V	"	"	"	
143	FJO 143V	"	Caetano C49F	1980	
144	FJO 144V	"	Caetano C53F	"	
145	FJO 145V	"	Caetano C49F	"	
146	GAU 727L	Leyland National 1051/2R	B40D	1973	(c)
147	NTV 734M	Leyland National 1151/2R	B48D	"	(d)
148	KUC 919F	Daimler 'Fleetline' CRL6	Metro-Cammell H44/27D	1975	(e)

Fleet No.	Regn. Number	Chassis Make and Type	Body Make and Seats	Date New	Notes
149	VUD 149X	Leyland 'Tiger' TRCTL11/3R	Plaxton C50F	1982	
150	VUD 150X	"	"	"	
151	VUD 151X	"	"	"	
152	KCR 103P	Leyland National 10351/2R	B40D	1976	(f)
153	KCR 111P	"	"	"	(f)
154	KCR 114P	"	"	"	(f)
155	OJD 228R	Leyland 'Fleetline' FE30AGR	Metro-Cammell H44/24D	1977	(g)
156	OJD 233R	"	"	"	(g)
157	OJD 201R	"	"	"	(g)
158	A158 PUD	Volvo B10M-	Jonckheere C51FT	1984	
159	B159 VJO	"	Jonckheere C49FT	1985	
160	OJD 244R	Leyland 'Fleetline' FE30AGR	Metro-Cammell H44/24D	1977	(h)
161	TGY 101M	Leyland National 1051/2R	B36D	1973	(h)

NOTES:-
(a) 127 (DAU 358C) was ex Nottingham City Transport No. 358 in 1977
(b) 140 (MLK 419L) was ex London Transport No. DMS419 in 1979
(c) 146 (GAU 727L) was ex Nottingham City Transport No. 727 in 1980
(d) 147 (NTV 734M) was ex Nottingham City Transport No. 734 in 1981
(e) 148 (KUC 919P) was ex London Transport No. DM1919 in 1981
(f) 152-154 (KCR 103/111/114P) were ex City of Portsmouth Passenger Transport Nos. 103/111/114 in 1982
(g) 155-157 (OJD 228/233/201R) were ex London Transport Nos. DMS2228/2233/2201 in 1983 (155/156) and 1984 (157)
(h) 160/161 (OJD 244R and TGY 101M) were ex London Buses Nos. DMS2244 and LS1 in 1985

H V Richmond Ltd

Mr A Livermore started this business in Barley, Hertfordshire, in the 1920s. The fleet contained examples of typical small buses in the 1930s period, including a Dodge, two Chevrolets, an Austin, a Ford and a succession of Bedfords. After Ford recommenced building full-sized PSVs in 1960, Richmond's bought many of these, and for many years the fleet was wholly standardised on Fords, although seven of the present fleet are of Volvo manufacture.

Mr Livermore sold the entire business, vehicles, services and all, to Mr H V Richmond in 1946. Mr Richmond continued to run the coach fleet as sole trader until the present limited company was incorporated in January 1979.

The company's larger neighbour, Premier Travel of Cambridge, whose operating base was at nearby Chrishall for many years, bought out Drayton's of Barley, with eight vehicles, in 1947, and thus acquired several rural services in the area. Nevertheless Richmond's continue their two stage carriage routes which operate on Wednesdays and Saturdays; the Royston - Kelsall - Sandon route on which Richmond's are the sole operator, and the Royston - Icknield Walk town service, shared with Premier Travel service 16. Richmond's run the town service on Wednesday and Saturday mornings, whilst Premier Travel takes over in the afternoons and also on Fridays. Recently Richmond's have introduced a Monday stage carriage service between Reed End, Kelshall, Sandon and Buntingford. A Barley - Hitchin cross-country run was also worked for some years but has now ceased.

Despite the rural nature of the area, Richmond's fleet has more than doubled, from 7 to 16 vehicles, during the last 20 years. The headquarters is at The Garage, Barley, near Royston. Fleet livery is cream and brown.

Regn. Number	Chassis Make and Type	Body Make and Seats	Date New	Notes
476 BTO	Volvo B10M-61	Plaxton C57F	1983	(a)
648 EAU	Ford R1114	Duple C53F	1979	(b)
275 FUM	Volvo B10M-61	Plaxton C57F	1982	(b)
753 LNV	Ford R1114	Plaxton C53F	1979	(b)
892 LTV	Ford R192	Plaxton C45F	1972	(c)
239 LYC	Volvo B10M-61	Plaxton C53F	1983	(b)
194 MDV	Ford R1114	Duple C53F	1980	(b)
403 NMM	Volvo B10M-61	Plaxton C57F	1982	(d)
668 PTM	"	Plaxton C53F	1983	(e)
426 YRA	Ford R1014	Plaxton C45F	1976	(f)
JNK 989N	Ford R1114	Plaxton C53F	1975	
CVS 957T	"	Duple C53F	1979	
PNM 673W	"	"	1980	
A220 PBM	Ford 'Transit'	Trimoco 12-seat	1984	
B29 ABH	Volvo B10M-61	Plaxton C53F	1985	
B618 AMD	"	"	1984	

NOTES:-
(a) 476 BTO was ex O'Connor, London W7, in 1985, and was re-registered ex RMU 964Y on acquisition
(b) 648 EAU, 275 FUM, 753 LNV, 239 LYC and 194 MDV were re-registered ex KRO 658V, OMM 675X, KRO 659V, TMG 671Y and PNM 674W respectively in 1984
(c) 892 LTV was ex N & S, Oadby, in 1975; it was re-registered ex FNR 9L in 1984
(d) 403 NMM was ex O'Connor, London W7, in 1984, and was re-registered ex VCX 411X in 1985
(e) 668 PTM was ex Ralph, Longford, in 1985, and was re-registered ex RMH 868Y on acquisition
(f) 426 YRA was ex AC, Bournemouth, in 1977; it was re-registered ex MRU 56P in 1984

Safeguard Coaches Ltd

Safeguard Coaches was founded by Arthur Newman, a coal and general haulier, who in 1924 had a charabanc body fitted to one of his Daimler lorries. In the next few years, seaside and racecourse excursions were operated, but in 1927 the first bus service was started, from Guildford to Aldershot Road Estate via Woodbridge Hill - a forerunner of the present Westborough route. Another service was soon started from Guildford to Onslow Village via Guildford Park. These activities brought the firm into trouble from Aldershot & District, who competed with Safeguard, in the custom of those times, by the use of 'chasers' and cutthroat fares competition. However, at the end of 1929 the two operators made an agreement which remained in force until recently, giving Safeguard a monopoly on the Aldershot Road Estate service, and Aldershot & District on Onslow Village. The two firms agreed to share the Guildford Park and later Dennisville service.

The present Limited Company was formed about 1933. Continuing housing development allowed Safeguard to extend their two routes to new termini at Park Barn, Northway and Dennisville (joint with Alder Valley). The Park Barn service operated by two separate routes ('A' via Westborough and 'B' via the Royal Surrey County Hospital) but apart from these the Safeguard routes were not identified by letters or numbers. The company also continues its involvement in the coaching business. Nowadays not only day excursions, but British and Continental extended tours, are run from the Guildford area.

Dennis buses and coaches, built locally in Guildford, were used by Safeguard for many years; but after 1948 orders switched to AEC for heavyweight stage buses, and to Bedfords for coaching duties (a number of Bedford service buses were also bought). The only double-decker ever used was a secondhand Guy 'Arab' which was tried on the Dennisville route from 1950 to 1952. From then until 1974 virtually nothing but AECs and Bedfords were bought, until the Leyland 'Leopard' replaced the AEC 'Reliance' as the basic service bus. The heavy loadings on the bus routes, especially on Westborough/Park Barn, dictated an early conversion to the 36-ft long single-decker; two long AEC 'Reliance' service buses bought in 1963/1964 were among the first of this type to be seen in the Guildford area.

The introduction of the 'Weyfarer' local network by the NBC companies in 1979, and the opening of the new Friary bus station in Guildford in 1980, greatly altered Safeguard's route network. All routes were transferred to run from the Friary, after many years split between the separate Farnham Road and Onslow Street bus stations. The Park Barn 'A' and 'B' routes were left largely unchanged, but the Northway route was surrendered, to be incorporated into an Alder Valley route. In exchange, the joint working with Alder Valley on the Dennisville route was extended to a cross-City route from the County Hospital to Bellfields Estate, an Alder Valley preserve since Aldershot and District had taken over Yellow Bus in 1958.

The April 1985 service revision in Guildford affected Safeguard as it did all other local operators. Park Barn services A/B have become G4/G5 under the new system, and the Dennisville - Bellfields through route has been curtailed to run from the Friary to Bellfields only (service G3), joint with Alder Valley; the Dennisville run, which Safeguard have been working since the start of their stage operations, is now part of service G5. In addition, a morning school journey, numbered G12, runs between Fairlands Estate and Park Barn School; Alder Valley provides the corresponding afternoon journey. The Onslow Village route, which Safeguard lost to Alder Valley under the 1929 agreement, has returned to the independent fold but is now worked by Blue Saloon as service G1.

The livery is red and cream (buses) and grey/red (coaches). The head office is adjacent to the depot at Guildford Park, and there is a booking and enquiry office at the Friary bus station in Guildford city centre. The Newman family still controls the company. For a fuller account of Safeguard's past, with fascinating illustrations and a full fleet history, the Diamond Jubilee book written by Messrs J Sutton and N Hamshere is recommended. It costs £1.80 post free from the Company or from the authors.

Regn. Number	Chassis Make and Type	Body Make and Seats	Date New	Notes
MPG 151P	Leyland 'Leopard' PSU3C/4R	Duple B53F	1976	
OPC 26R	"	"	"	
UGB 14R	AEC 'Reliance' 6U3ZR	"	1977	(a)
TPL 166S	Bedford YMT	"	1977	
DPD 33T	Bedford YLQ	Duple C45F	1979	
YPB 839T	Leyland 'Leopard' PSU3E/4R	Plaxton C49F	"	
FPA 584V	"	"	"	
GFG 342V	"	Duple B53F	1980	
NPD 689W	"	"	1981	
NPD 690W	Bedford YNT	Plaxton C53F	"	
SPH 13X	Ford 'Transit'	Tricentrol 12-seat	"	
TPA 968X	Leyland 'Leopard' PSU3F/4R	Duple B53F	"	
UPG 349X	Leyland 'Tiger' TRCTL11/3R	Plaxton C53F	1982	
YPD 217Y	Leyland 'Leopard' PSU3G/4R	Duple B53F	"	
APF 617Y	Bedford YNT	Plaxton C53F	1983	

Regn. Number	Chassis Make and Type	Body Make and Seats	Date New	Notes
BPC 227Y	Bedford YNT	Plaxton C49F	1983	
UTN 956Y	Leyland 'Tiger' TRCTL11/3R	Plaxton C51F	"	(b)
A60 FPD	Bedford YNT	Plaxton C49F	1984	
A61 FPD	"	Plaxton C53F	"	
A60 GPL	Mercedes-Benz L608D	Reeves Burgess C19F	"	
A62 HPG	Leyland 'Tiger' TRCTL11/3R	Plaxton C53F	"	
B717 MPC	"	Duple C51F	1985	

NOTES:-
(a) UCB 14R was ex Tillingbourne, Chilworth, in 1985
(b) UTN 956Y was ex Moor-Dale, Newcastle-upon-Tyne, in 1985

Smith's (Buntingford) Ltd

The founder of this firm, Wilfred Smith, was the son of the proprietor of a furnishing and hardware store at 18 High Street, Buntingford. The horse-drawn delivery wagon being off the road due to shortage of horses (which had probably been impressed by the Army during the First World War), Wilfred learnt to drive a Model T Ford motor van at the age of 12! From about 1921 the van was also used to take passengers to Hitchin market, and for a few years Bishop's Stortford was also served. Regular bus operations were started in the late 1920s with a Crossley tender bought from the Royal Flying Corps, which was succeeded about 1930 by a Lancia 14-seater coach bought from Southern National.

The main Buntingford - Hitchin route was licensed under the Road Traffic Act of 1930. Although it was wholly within the LPTB Area, the Board did not want to acquire it as it was known to be uneconomic. Thus the Smith's were left working the route, which ran six days a week until the post-war years, when falling passenger demand caused a reduction to market day and Saturday operation. Another service, to Letchworth, ran five days a week as late as 1966.

Nowadays there is a service on Tuesdays and Saturdays only to Hitchin via Weston, and on the same days from Therfield (Tuesdays) and Buntingford (Saturdays) to Hitchin via Baldock; on Mondays and Fridays a service runs from Dane End to Buntingford. This much reduced timetable is operated mainly by coaches, although two service buses - the Bedford VAS and the ex-London Transport Bristol LH - are available for these duties if required.

In 1982 Smith's took over the Braughing - Bishop's Stortford service of B C Cannon Ltd of Puckeridge. After the death of Cannon's managing director, Mr W J Mansfield, in 1982, his executors abandoned the service and Smith's took it over one week later. Under Smith's management the service runs from Buntingford to Bishop's Stortford via Braughing; there are two round trips on Thursdays only (Bishop's Stortford was given on Thursdays). Thus Smith's have re-entered Bishop's Stortford over 50 years after they abandoned their own short-lived service in the 1920s; and just 50 years after B C Cannon had started the Braughing route.

After the Lancia, the prewar fleet included a Ford, two Dodges and two Bedfords. One of the latter was bought secondhand from an Isle of Wight operator with the registration CDL 693. This started Smith's 'trademark' of registering all new vehicles with the digits '693'. This policy started with LNK 693, the last Bedford OE delivered in 1950, and it still continues, although the pattern is spoiled by the registrations of secondhand vehicles. Since 1950, the registrations

NJH 693, 693 NJH and NJH 693D have all been used on Smith's coaches.

A new Thurgood-bodied Guy 'Arab' Mk III arrived in 1946, while a similar body was fitted to a Leyland 'Cheetah' LZ4 delivered in 1948! The Cheetah had in fact been built prewar, and its chassis was used during the war to carry an Army searchlight unit; it was sold to Smith's by the War Department and was bodied after the war. Otherwise, the postwar fleet was mainly of Bedford and Ford manufacture until recently when heavyweight vehicles began to appear; the fleet is now more varied than for some time, with six makes (AEC, Bedford, Bristol, Ford, Mercedes-Benz and Volvo) represented, of which Bedford and Ford account for only one apiece.

The traditional livery of blue and ivory has been replaced since 1980 by a yellow, brown and orange colour scheme which was inspired by the livery of ex-Surrey Motors AEC 'Reliance' EGS 156T. The base of operations is at Station Road, Buntingford.

Regn. Number	Chassis Make and Type	Body Make and Seats	Date New	Notes
958 VKM	Volvo B58-61	Plaxton C53F	1980	(a)
KPU 262J	Bedford VAS2	Marshall B28F	1970	(b)
KJD 438P	Bristol LH6L	ECW B39F	1976	(c)
OEB 693R	AEC 'Reliance' 6U2R	Plaxton C57F	1977	
SVA 693S	AEC 'Reliance' 6U3ZR	"	1978	
CTM 418T	"	"	1979	(d)
EGS 156T	"	Plaxton C46F	"	(e)
VJY 922V	Volvo B58-61	Plaxton C53F	1980	(a)
XPP 693X	Volvo B10M-61		1981	
GJN 661Y	Ford 'Transit'	Ford/Smith 12-seat	1982	(f)
A693 NBM	Volvo B10M-61	Plaxton C49FT	1983	(g)
B693 BGS	Mercedes-Benz 608D	Ensor C21F	1985	

NOTES:-
(a) 958 VKM and VJY 922V were ex Felicita, Gillingham, in 1983; 958 VKM was re-registered ex VJY 921V in 1985
(b) KPU 262J was ex Essex Police, Chelmsford, No. P393 (non-PSV) in 1978
(c) KJD 438P was ex London Transport No. BL38 in 1983
(d) CTM 418T was ex Iberian, London W8, in 1981
(e) EGS 156T was ex Surrey Motors, Sutton, in 1980
(f) GJN 661Y was ex Ford Motor Co, Brentwood, in 1984
(g) A693 NBM is based on the chassis of STT 608X, new to Trathen, Yelverton No. 08 in 1981 with a Van Hool C49FT body. The Van Hool body was destroyed by fire and the chassis was acquired by Smith's for rebodying. The Plaxton body was fitted in 1983

S J and A M Tate

In 1926 Messrs Barnard and Bedford set up shop in Potten End with a 14-seater Chevrolet bus, trading as B & B Services. In 1933, by which time Mr Barnard was in sole charge, Mr J Bright (Village Services Bus) was taken over with two vehicles, including another Chevrolet. Since then B & B and its successors, Tates, have provided all the bus services of Potten End village.

The fleet in the early days was made up of Chevrolet, Reo, Gilford and BAT machines, and a Commer was bought new as late as 1949. After then the B & B fleet standardised on Bedfords. B & B ran one of the last wartime utility Bedford OWB models remaining in service in the Metropolitan Traffic Area.

In 1961 Mr Barnard retired, and handed over the business to his fitter, Mr P J W Reid, the nephew of the late Mr J R G Dell of Rover Bus Service, Chesham. Mr Reid remained in charge until 21st May 1979, when control passed to S J and A M Tate, of Tate's Coaches of Markyate. The Potten End business continued as a separate unit from the old address, using the traditional 'B & B Services' fleetname. Early signs of the change of management were the replacement of the Bell Punch ticket system with Setright ticket machines, and the change of livery from red and cream to blue and cream. In August 1983 the two businesses were merged. The united enterprise is run from Tate's old headquarters at 144 High Street, Markyate; but the depot at Water End Road, Potten End, provides vehicles for the stage services which still trade under the 'B & B' fleetname. Recently four Bova coaches have been bought, contrasting with the traditional Bedford and Ford vehicles.

The main service runs six days a week from Potten End to Berkhamsted, with occasional extensions to Aldbury. The service from Potten End to Hemel Hempstead now runs three or four trips daily from Berkhamsted to Hemel Hempstead via Hudnall Common and Potten End, with several alternative routeings on different days of the week.

Regn. Number	Chassis Make and Type	Body Make and Seats	Date New	Notes
DPV 881	Bova EL26/581	Bova C53F	1981	(a)
VLV 815	"	Duple C53F	1985	
209 DYB	Ford R1014	Plaxton C37F	1978	(b)
975 FYB	Bova EL26/581	Bova C53F	1983	(b)
STT 411R	Bristol LHL6L	ECW B43F	1977	(c)
VNM 239S	Bedford YLQ	Duple C45F	"	
VPN 6S	Bedford YMT	Plaxton C53F	"	(d)
MWU 186V	"	"	1980	(e)
RKX 26W	Bedford YMQ	Plaxton C45F	"	
JTC 780X	Bova EL26/581	Bova C53F	1982	(f)

NOTES:-
(a) DPV 881 was ex Bonas, Coventry, in 1984; it was re-registered ex URW 702X in 1984
(b) 209 DYB and 975 FYB were re-registered ex CBM 296T and HBH 906Y respectively in 1984
(c) STT 411R was ex Devon General Omnibus Co No. 119 in 1985
(d) VPN 6S was ex Moon, Sheepshed, in 1981
(e) MWU 186V was ex Belle Vue, Wakefield, No. 23 in 1983
(f) JTC 780X was ex Globe, Warmley, in 1985

Telling's Coaches of Weybridge Ltd

Telling's Coaches was founded by Mr S R Telling at Broadwater Farm, Thames Street, Weybridge, in May 1974. For the first couple of years Mr Telling's enterprise remained a one-vehicle business, but the fleet size then began to grow, mainly standardising on Bedford vehicles.

In 1980 the first Volvo owned by the fleet was bought secondhand from Golden Miller of Feltham. In May 1981 Telling's took over the two-vehicle business of Jubilee Coaches Ltd of Chertsey. The present fleet is standardised on front-line Volvo coaches except for a Ford 'Transit' and two Mercedes-Benz 21-seaters. The secondhand purchase of the Volvo from Golden Miller foreshadowed the recent takeover by Telling's of F G Wilder Ltd (Golden Miller Coaches) in 1985.

The history of Golden Miller began in 1923, when Mr F G Wilder started a haulage business with compensation received after a serious accident. The business concentrated on contract hire to a few large customers, one of whom collapsed in the early 1950s, driving Mr Wilder's firm to the brink of bankruptcy itself; but it survived, and in 1955 commenced passenger operation, buying a Bedford OE coach.

In the same year Fred Varney's 'Golden Miller' business was acquired, with two coaches and a Twickenham booking office, giving Wilder's their present fleetname. In 1967 Tourist Bus Service was acquired, with one vehicle and a licence for a service from Feltham Station to East Bedfont (now service 601); this route had been the first privately-run bus route since the war to receive London Transport's consent, in 1955. On 1st January 1968 two further services were started, from Feltham to Shepperton Station (service 602) and to Hanworth (service 603). In November 1970 the Walton-on-Thames to Walton Station service of Walton-on-Thames Motor Co Ltd, which had begun in 1923 and was never taken over by the LPTB, was acquired by Golden Miller and extended to Oatlands Village; however, this route (604) was not a success and was withdrawn. Service number 605 was meant for a route planned but not introduced in Claygate; while 606 was started in 1971 between Staines and Stanwellmoor, separated from the rest of the network, whose other three routes meet at Feltham Station. Golden Miller acquired the coaching business of Beach of Staines in 1977, bringing the firm into the field of express service operation for the first time.

In April 1985, following the Telling's takeover, a substantial service reduction took place; service 602 was thinned down to four journeys a day, and school journeys in the Stanwellmoor area on service 606 were transferred to London Country Bus Services as services 605/606.

The fleet livery is blue and buff (Golden Miller) and cream/blue (Telling's). The main office and garage for the group is at Telling's premises at Wintersells Road, Byfleet; there is also a garage and office at the Golden Miller premises at Fern Grove, Feltham. In the lists which follow, ownership of each vehicle is indicated by the code TE (Telling's Coaches of Weybridge Ltd) or GM (F G Wilder Ltd - Golden Miller Coaches) in the left-hand column.

Fleet	Regn. Number	Chassis Make and Type	Body Make and Seats	Date New	Notes
GM	NLJ 827G	Bristol RELL6G	ECW DP50F	1969	(a)
GM	FVX 614H	"	ECW B53F	"	(b)
GM	POD 826H	"	"	"	(c)
GM	TUO 255J	"	"	1970	(c)
GM	LNN 93K	Bristol RELH6G	ECW DP47F	1972	(d)
TE	SMF 774S	Ford 'Transit'	Dormobile B16F	1977	(e)
TE	SDR 440T	Volvo B58-61	Plaxton C50F	1979	(f)
TE	NLC 873V	"	Plaxton C57F	1980	(g)
TE	XRP 761W	"	Jonckheere C51FT	1981	(h)
TE	ONV 649Y	Volvo B10M-61	"	1983	(i)
TE	ONV 651Y	"	"	"	(i)
TE	ONV 652Y	"	"	"	(i)
GM	B916 BGA	"	Van Hool C53F	1985	
GM	B917 BGA	"	"	"	
TE	B510 CBD	"	Jonckheere C53F	"	
TE	B520 CBD	"	Jonckheere C51FT	1984	(j)
GM	B998 CUS	"	Van Hool C53F	1985	
GM	C334 FSU	"	Van Hool C42FT	"	
GM	C335 FSU	"	"	"	
GM	C336 FSU	"	"	"	
TE	C337 FSU	Mercedes-Benz L608D	Reeves Burgess C21F	"	
TE	C338 FSU	"	Mellor C21F	"	

NOTES:—
(a) NLJ 827G was ex Dulieu, Dagenham, in 1985
(b) FVX 614H was ex Eastern National Omnibus Co No. 1512 in 1985
(c) POD 826H and TUO 255J were ex Devon General Nos. 2727/2743 in 1985
(d) LNN 93K was ex East Midland Motor Services No. 93 in 1985
(e) SMF 774S was ex American Schools, London SW7 No. 126 in 1980
(f) SDR 440T was ex Trathen, Yelverton in 1982, and is named 'The Miss Michelle'
(g) NLC 873V was ex Albatross, Isleworth in 1982
(h) XRP 761W was ex J E Stockdale, Selby in 1983
(i) ONV 649/651/652Y were ex NAT, Leeds in 1985
(j) B520 CBD was delivered new to Telling, but the order was diverted from Rapson, Brora

Thames Weald Ltd

When London Transport (Country Area) withdrew several services in August 1961, Mr Cranley Onslow, then a rural district councillor, organised a fortnightly hired coach between the North-West Kent village of Fawkham Green, and Gravesend. Almost immediately Dr H N Heffernan, a local resident, took over the arrangements and identified several other unserved settlements in the inaccessible Otford Hills area. By September he was enrolling potential passengers in the Thames Weald Travel Society, and linking all these hamlets by a through twice-weekly service between Sevenoaks and Gravesend. By December 1961 Dr Heffernan held a Road Service Licence for this 21-mile route, but was prohibited from carrying through passengers from end to end, and still did not have a vehicle of his own.

In May 1962 the 'On Hire' signs came down as Dr Heffernan's own 12-seater Commer minibus came on to the route. It was later replaced by a 13-seater diesel Trojan, styled as a scaled-down version of a full-size coach. The undertaking was incorporated as Thames Weald Ltd in December 1962, and two larger 'midi' vehicles were bought. The first, a Bedford J2SZ 20-seater, was based on a modified goods chassis and turned out to be a 'boneshaker'; the second, a Bedford VAS 29-seater, remained as the 'flagship' of the fleet for a full 20 years, lending capacity to services which were otherwise operated by 12-seat and 16-seat Ford 'Transits'. A 26-seat ex-London Transport GS (Guy 'Vixen') was owned for a while; to get it round some of the bends in the lanes was an exercise in precision driving!

When London Transport discontinued the Dartford Tunnel services in 1967, Thames Weald switched its main service to provide a cross-river link from Sevenoaks to Romford on a two-hourly frequency, with Gravesend still served by a connecting branch. From 1971 to 1973, the main line was extended at the other end to run from Romford to Crawley, at 65 miles one of the longest stage services in the country. This extension was withdrawn at the time of the prohibitive rise in the price of motor fuel in the early 1970s.

Thames Weald now operates two Rootes-bodied Dodges bought after a spell as demonstrators. The present Monday to Friday service comprises peak-hour journeys between West Kingsdown and Sevenoaks, extended to and from Longfield, Hartley and New Ash Green during school term; eight schools in the Sevenoaks area are served. The Sevenoaks - Romford route runs on Wednesdays, Thursdays and Fridays; a Maidstone - Romford service runs on Saturdays. There is also a monthly excursion covering the original Gravesend route. Some expansion of the Maidstone service is envisaged for the future.

In the Birthday Honours of June 1985, H M The Queen appointed Dr Heffernan an MBE "for services to community transport in Kent".

The headquarters of the company is at Fawkham Road, West Kingsdown, Kent.

Regn. Number	Chassis Make and Type	Body Make and Seats	Date New	Notes
JKR 238V	Dodge RB56	Rootes B23F	1980	(a)
PKR 399W	Dodge S66-C	Rootes DP27F	1981	(b)

NOTES:-
(a) JKR 238V was ex Rootes demonstrator in 1980
(b) PKR 399W was ex Rootes demonstrator in 1982

Tillingbourne Bus Co Ltd

Mr G Trice, the village carrier of Chilworth, Surrey, ran a horse and cart which was the village's only public transport in the early years of the present century. Passengers rode on the tailboard of the cart! However, in 1924 Mr Trice went into the motorbus business, trading as 'Tillingbourne Valley Services'. In early 1928 there was a disastrous fire at Mr Trice's premises, and most of the fleet was lost; but he painstakingly built up the business again, basing it on purchases of four new 14-seater Chevrolets, the standard lightweight bus of the period.

In 1930 Mr Trice agreed to share traffic with his larger neighbours, East Surrey Traction and Aldershot & District, between whose areas his service ran. The agreement, from 1st December 1930, regulated the times of the two big companies, Tillingbourne Valley and Mr A R Rudall's 'Magnet' Service on Guildford - Peaslake service 44 (later 448). In 1934 Tillingbourne Valley avoided takeover by the LPTB, which had refused consent for local passengers to be carried in Guildford. The Board backed down in the face of protests from Tillingbourne passengers, and granted consent annually until 1969 when it ceased to be required.

Mr Trice died in 1933, leaving the business to his son, another G Trice, and his son-in-law Mr L Rhees. The latter was soon bought out but set up his own business, 'Tillingbourne Valley Coaches', nearby. The main business continued to concentrate on bus services - no coach-bodied vehicles were owned until 1950. Services ran from Guildford to Farley Green, Peaslake, and a short Guildford town service (withdrawn in 1971) to Warren Road. Tillingbourne Valley Bus Co Ltd was incorporated in 1935, and was renamed Tillingbourne Valley Services Ltd in 1936.

Pre-war buses were mainly Thornycrofts, but the last of these arrived in 1946. Austins and Bedfords, mostly bought secondhand, followed them. The company bought 8 ex-London Transport GS-type Guy 'Vixens' with ECW 26-seat bodies in 1963/1964; some remained until 1970, although by then some had been replaced by Bristol SC4LKs. A third generation of Trices, Mr G T Trice and Mrs M E Trice, took over in 1950 and were soon fighting rival takeover bids from London Transport (again) and the Hants & Sussex empire, then at the height of its power. In 1964, London Transport gave up its share of the 448 route for a small payment by Tillingbourne, leaving the latter company to run the whole service to Ewhurst.

In 1970 the Trices sold out to T J W and J C Brown, the present directors, and soon afterwards the name was changed to Tillingbourne Bus Co Ltd. Subsidiary companies were set up as Tillingbourne (Sussex) Ltd, and Tillingbourne (Metropolitan) Ltd, the latter created in July 1981 to work the services acquired from Orpington & District in March 1981.

The headquarters of the parent company was moved from New Road, Chilworth, to the station yard at Gomshall. This location was not ideal, and in March 1981 the company moved again to premises at Little Mead, Cranleigh. The new management also changed the livery from maroon and cream to the present blue, off-white and yellow; and bought full-sized 36-ft low vehicles for the first time, many of them coming new. Coaching nowadays is a sizeable proportion of the company's business.

As noted above, after Orpington & District ceased operations in early 1981, Tillingbourne stepped in on 2nd March 1981 with replacement services covering O & D's main route from East Croydon to Orpington (numbered 353 by Tillingbourne) and the branch to the Forestdale Estate (355/357). In September 1983 the Orpington services and some assets were sold to a new company, Metrobus Ltd., who still operate them and are featured separately in this book. In November 1982, the routes and some vehicles of Tony McCann Coaches Ltd of Forest Green were taken over by Tillingbourne. McCann's were successors to the old-established Brown Motor Services; they contributed a Forest Green – Guildford route, school journeys from Cranleigh to Dorking (444) and a Forest Green – Horsham route which was diverted to run from Cranleigh to Horsham via Ewhurst and Ockley, on Tuesdays, Fridays and Saturdays only. McCann's still operate a few local contracts and private hire with a much reduced fleet.

The Guildford service revisions of April 1985 gave Tillingbourne a virtual monopoly of operation in the villages lying in the angle between the Dorking and Cranleigh roads. All routes were re-numbered with two-figure numbers, which in some cases recall those under which the services were started many years ago. The present routes are 22 ('Tillingbourne Villager') from Ranmore and Dorking to Shere with connections to Guildford; 23/25 (Guildford – Wonersh – Cranleigh – Shere – Guildford circular); 33 (Guildford – Grafham – Cranleigh, extended on Sundays to Ewhurst); 44 (Cranleigh – Shere – Merrow – Guildford); 50/53 (Cranleigh – Warnham – Horsham); 51 (Horsham – North Heath circular); 52 (Horsham – Lambs Green); and 54 (Alfold – Horsham). Most of these routes are not frequent (except for 51 which works every 30 minutes most of the day); but they do serve some very attractive areas. For tourists (and enthusiasts!) wishing to tour the area by Tillingbourne bus, the company offers a Day Out ticket, for unlimited travel after 0900 on Mondays to Fridays, or all day Saturdays and Sundays; the fare was £1.90 for adults and 95p for children as we went to press.

The Tillingbourne group still comprises three companies:- Tillingbourne Bus Co Ltd., Tillingbourne (Sussex) Ltd. and Tillingbourne (Metropolitan) Ltd., all three of which hold PSV Operators' Licences. However, there is no fixed allocation of vehicles to the three companies, and no attempt has been made to show each vehicle 'belonging' to one company in the following list.

Regn. Number	Chassis Make and Type	Body Make and Seats	Date New	Notes
UGB 12R	AEC 'Reliance' 6U3ZR	Duple B53F	1977	(a)
CPG 160T	"	Plaxton C53F	1979	
CCG 550V	Bedford YMT	Duple B61F	1980	
JTM 109V	AEC 'Reliance' 6U2R	Duple B53F	1979	(b)
JDE 189X	Leyland 'Tiger' TRCTL11/2R	Duple C53F	1982	(c)
TTA 650X	Dennis 'Lancet' SD502	Wadham Stringer B52F	1981	
XTT 5X	Dennis 'Lancet' SD507	"	1982	
FOD 941Y	Bedford YNT	Plaxton B55F	1983	
FOD 942Y	Dennis 'Dorchester' SDA802	Wadham Stringer B61F	"	
FOD 943Y	"	"	"	
A889 FPM	Bedford YMT	Duple B55F	1984	
B327 KPD	Bedford YNT	Plaxton B53F	"	
B877 OLJ	Leyland 'Tiger' TRBTL11/?R	Duple B55F	"	
B124 PEL	Bedford YNT	Plaxton C53F	"	
B49 TVR	Ford 'Transit'	Dixon Lomas C16F	1985	

NOTES:-
(a) UGB 12R was ex Hutchison, Overtown, in 1985
(b) JTM 109V was new to Tillingbourne, but was on long-term lease to Metrobus

Ltd, Green Street Green, from 1983 to 1985 when it was returned
(c) JDE 189X was ex Silcox, Pembroke Dock No. 156 in 1985

Tourmaster Group

The Tricentrol group's nucleus was Luton Commercial Motors Ltd of Dunstable, whose main work was PSV conversion and sale of minibuses. In 1972 LCM was renamed Tricentrol PSV Sales Ltd. The Tricentrol group continued to produce PSV conversion for minibuses such as the Ford 'Transit' and Bedford CF, as well as complete bodies for types such as the Ford A-type midibus. In 1976 a new company, Tricentrol Chassis Developments Ltd, was formed; they offered major rebuilds of standard full-sized Bedford chassis, including a shortened 35-seat version on the YLQ and YMQ chassis, and a lengthened 12-metre version on the YMT and its successors. These modified chassis were sold widely, including some delivered to the coach operating companies in the Tricentrol group.

The Group soon made several takeovers far from its Dunstable base, well in the Leicestershire area. Tricentrol took control of Housden's and Caldwell's Coaches, both of Loughborough, in 1972, amalgamating them into Housden-Caldwell Coaches. In 1980 the Group also took over Howlett's of Quorn, an old-established company with both coaching and stage carriage work. Housden-Caldwell and Howlett's remained separate subsidiaries until March 1985, when they were merged under the Housden-Caldwell name. Several non-standard vehicles taken over from the independent Howlett's company remained in stock at the time of the 1985 merger, although Housden-Caldwell's rolling stock had been made up of Tourmaster standard types for some years before that. Housden-Caldwell still runs several stage carriage services in the Loughborough area as successors to Howlett's, and owns one Leyland 'Leopard' service bus for this work.

In 1974 Tricentrol took over North Star Coaches of Stevenage, a family firm just short of its 50th birthday. It had been founded by Mr W T Candler in July 1924, with a 14-seater Ford Model 'T' waggonette which ran a bus service between Stevenage and Hitchin. This route was highly competitive, but eventually North Star was running three buses on it. In 1934 the newly-formed LPTB decided not to purchase the North Star service, and the firm's buses ran on until October 1939 when the Candler family sold the buses voluntarily to the LPTB so as to concentrate on coaching. After the Fords, many Dennis vehicles were bought by North Star; after the war the coach business was built up so that a fleet of front-line coaches, mostly Bedfords, was passed to the Tricentrol group in 1974. A new company, North Star Travel Ltd, with headquarters at the Letchmere Road premises of the former company, was created by Tricentrol to control the North Star business, and North Star Coaches Ltd became defunct. North Star Travel Ltd was retained as a separate company within the larger group until December 1983; its address was moved to 4 Letchmere Road, Stevenage, in May 1981.

In 1975 Tricentrol acquired Travel House of Dunstable, which had been owned by the Costin family for many years. The business was founded by T W Blake of Dunstable before the Second World War; it passed to Dunstable Coaches Ltd in 1946 and then to H & H Motorways Ltd (Bunty Coachways) of Coventry. The Coventry firm sold it to Travel House (Luton) Ltd, the Costin family's travel agency, in 1951. Travel House had dabbled in stage carriage operation, with a licence to run from Dunstable to Luton Town football ground on match days! Under Tricentrol management the company's headquarters was moved to the Tricentrol head office at Tavistock Street, Dunstable. 15 Bedford and Ford coaches, including one Ford 'Transit' minibus, were involved in the takeover. In March 1981 Travel House (Luton) Ltd ceased trading and its operations were taken over by Tricentrol Coaches Ltd, the

Tricentrol group 'flagship'. Another subsidiary company, Milton Keynes Coaches Ltd of Leighton Buzzard, had its headquarters moved to the group head office at Dunstable in 1975.

In October 1982 Tricentrol Coaches Ltd was renamed Tourmaster Coaches Ltd, and this name has become both the name of the group and the principal fleetname.

The Group's main function is extended touring work and also private hire. However, Tourmaster has also participated in the National Express service between London (Victoria) and Milton Keynes, the Group's only regular express service working.

In the lists which follow, the codes shown are used to denote the company to which each vehicle is allocated; the operating base of each company is also shown:-
HC - Housden-Caldwell Coaches Ltd, 7 Wards End, Loughborough (also at Coalville)
MK - Milton Keynes Coaches Ltd, Tavistock Street, Dunstable
TO - Tourmaster Coaches Ltd, Tavistock Street, Dunstable

Fleet	Regn. Number	Chassis Make and Type	Body Make and Seats	Date New	Notes
HC	PVV 312	Bova EL26/581	Bova C52F	1983	(a)
HC	PVV 313	"	"	"	(a)
TO	PVV 314	DAF MB200DKTL600	Caetano C53F	"	(a)
HC	PVV 315	"	"	"	(a)
TO	PVV 316	Bova EL26/581	Bova C52F	"	(a)
TO	PVV 318	"	"	"	(a)
TO	WNO 481	Bristol KSW5G	ECW O33/28R	1953	(b)
HC	YRC 420	AEC 'Reliance' 6U3ZR	Plaxton C44FT	1978	(c)(a)
HC	517 ABT	Bova EL26/581	Bova C52F	1982	
TO	479 DKH	Bedford/Tricentrol YNT	Plaxton C57F	"	
HC	397 EFW	AEC 'Reliance' 6U2R	"	1977	(e)
HC	366 EKH	Bova EL26/581	Bova C52F	1982	(d)
TO	409 FRH	"	"	"	(d)
HC	926 FRH	"	Bova C48FT	"	(d)
HC	682 FUV	DAF MB200DKFL600	Plaxton C57F	1983	(a)
HC	997 GAT	Bova EL26/581	Bova C52F	1981	
HC	885 NBH	DAF MB200	Caetano C53F	1984	(e)
TO	893 PTJ	Bova EL26/581	Bova C52F	1982	(d)
HC	426 VNU	Bedford YNT	Plaxton C53F	1984	(e)
HC	866 VNU	"	"	"	(e)
HC	KUT 587P	Leyland 'Leopard' PSU3C/4R	Duple B66F	1975	
HC	LVS 232P	Ford R1114	Plaxton C53F	1976	
MK	BMJ 508T	Bedford YMT	Duple C53F	1978	
TO	BMJ 512T	"	"	"	
TO	DNK 434T	Ford R1114	"	1979	
HC	DNK 437T	Bedford YMT	"	"	
TO	FKX 154T	"	Duple C44F	"	
HC	FKX 156T	"	Duple C53F	"	
HC	JBH 381V	"	"	"	
TO	JBH 383V	"	"	"	
TO	JBH 385V	"	Duple C34F	"	
TO	JVS 286V	Bedford YNT	Plaxton C53F	1978	(g)
MK	MMJ 537V	Bedford YMT	Duple C53F	1980	
TO	MMJ 544V	"	"	"	
MK	MMJ 546V	"	"	"	
MK	MMJ 547V	"	"	"	
TO	MMJ 549V	"	"	"	
HC	NRO 261V	Bedford/Tricentrol YMT	Duple C57F	"	
HC	PNM 693W	Bedford YLQ	Duple C45F	"	
HC	PNM 695W	Bedford/Tricentrol YMQ	Duple C35F	1981	
HC	PNM 696W	Ford 'Transit'	Tricentrol 12-seat	1980	
HC	UMJ 415W	Bedford YNT	Duple C53F	1981	

55

Fleet	Regn. Number	Chassis Make and Type	Body Make and Seats	Date New	Notes
HC	UMJ 416W	Bedford YNT	Duple C53F	1981	
HC	UMJ 417W	"	"	"	
TO	UMJ 418W	"	"	"	
HC	UMJ 419W	"	Duple C34F	"	
MK	UMJ 420W	"	Duple C53F	"	
TO	UMJ 424W	Bedford YMT	"	"	
HC	UMJ 426W	"	"	"	
HC	UMJ 427W	"	"	"	
HC	UMJ 428W	"	"	"	
TO	WBM 47X	Bedford YN1	"	"	
HC	WBM 48X	"	Duple C46F	"	
TO	WBM 49X	Bedford/Tricentrol YMT	Duple C57F	"	
TO	ABH 773X	Bedford YNT	Duple C53F	1982	
HC	A256 SBM	Bova 'Futura' FHD12-280	Bova C49FT	1984	
HC	A258 SBM	"	"	"	
HC	B244 YKX	Bova EL29-581	Bova C53F	1985	
HC	B245 YKX	"	"	"	
HC	B247 YKX	"	"	"	
MK	B250 YKX	"	"	"	
HC	B252 YKX	"	"	"	
HC	B253 YKX	"	"	"	

NOTES:-
(a) PVV 312-316/318, YRC 420, 682 FUV were re-registered ex JRO 613/614Y, CAY 215/214Y, JRO 612/616Y, ANR 900T, DVS 163Y in 1983
(b) WNO 481 was ex Silverline, Hounslow, in 1975
(c) YRC 420 is used by Leicester City Football Club and is named 'Cityliner'
(d) 366 EKH, 409/926 FRH, 893 PTJ were re-registered ex WMJ 377X, CTM 779X, AMJ 791X, CTM 780X in 1982
(e) 397 EFW, 885 NBH, 426/866 VNU were re-registered ex RJU 406R, A196 FAY, A254/253 SBM in 1983
(g) JVS 286V was ex Vauxhall Motors, Luton, in 1982
Vehicles shown as of 'Bedford/Tricentrol' manufacture were either shortened (YLQ and YMQ) or lengthened (YMT) by Tricentrol Chassis Developments prior to bodying

Whyte's Airport Services Ltd

Whyte's Airport Services is now responsible for most of the 'airside' buses which ferry passengers between flights at Heathrow Airport. A much larger operation which included links for airport workers and visitors on the 'landside', i.e. public, areas of the Airport, was closed in 1981 when the British Airports Authority gave the services to Ralph's Coaches of Colnbrook, who are featured separately in this book. Similarly, the Rail-Air service from Feltham BR Station to Heathrow Airport, which was the first public bus service to operate through the southern approach tunnel to the Airport terminal area, has also been discontinued.

Mr Leslie Whyte entered the coaching world in 1960, running one coach in his spare time to supplement his income from the Civil Service. Evidently he was successful, for before long he gave up his Civil Service career to become a full-time coach proprietor. The business was based at Edgware and the firm was registered as Whyte's (Edgware) Ltd.